INVEST LIKE THE BEST

INVEST LIKE

THE LOW-RISK **ROAD TO** HIGH RETURNS

CHRIS BELCHAMBER

LIONCREST
PUBLISHING

INVEST LIKE THE BEST

The Low-Risk Road to High Returns

ISBN   978-1-5445-1876-3 *Hardcover*

        978-1-5445-1875-6 *Paperback*

        978-1-5445-1874-9 *Ebook*

I can't thank my support team enough for their endless help while writing this book. My sister Clare Martin, my son Daniel Belchamber, and my fiancée Mary Duffus.

I must also express my deep gratitude to everyone mentioned in this book for their great inspiration and education.

"If I have seen further, it is by standing on the shoulders of Giants."

—SIR ISAAC NEWTON, 1675

CONTENTS

BOOK DISCLAIMER 9

INTRODUCTION 11

PART I: DEVELOP A BEST INVESTORS MINDSET

1. BE FULLY AWARE OF THE INVESTMENT CHALLENGE 23

2. AVOID SELF-SABOTAGE: BUILD AN INVESTMENT MINDSET FRAMEWORK 35

3. BENEFIT FROM SYSTEMATIC INVESTING...49

4. AVOID MISDIRECTION: WHAT CAN HAPPEN IF YOU JUST CHASE RETURNS 61

PART II: RISK AND RETURN, DYNAMIC COMPOUNDING, AND ASSESSMENT

5. BEST INVESTORS ARE CRYSTAL CLEAR ABOUT PRIORITIES AND METRICS 81

6. MASTER THE ESSENTIAL MATH OF INVESTING: DYNAMIC COMPOUND INTEREST 95

7. EMPOWER YOURSELF THROUGH MEASUREMENT 117

8. KNOW THE INVESTMENT MYTHS AND HERESIES WITH BEST INVESTOR ANALYSIS....129

PART III: INVEST LIKE THE BEST

9. MONEY MANAGEMENT MATTERS..147

10. INVESTMENT ALLOCATION 157

11. ACTIVE INVESTMENT MANAGEMENT..167

12. DECISIVE COMPREHENSIVE PROCEDURE FOR CONSISTENT PERFORMANCE 177

CONCLUSION..189

ABOUT THE AUTHOR...201

BOOK DISCLAIMER

The opinions expressed in this commentary are those of the author. This is for general information only and is not intended to provide specific investment advice or recommendations for any individual, and nothing contained herein should be construed as legal or tax advice. Before implementing any strategies, you need to seek proper financial, legal, and accounting counsel.

This book may contain forward-looking statements based on hypothetical assumptions, estimates, outlook, and other judgments made in light of information available at the time it was written and involve both known and unknown risks and uncertainties. Accordingly, plans, goals, and other statements may not be realized as described, and actual financial results and success/failure may differ materially from those presented herein.

Depending on your individual circumstances, the strategies presented may not be appropriate for your situation. Please consult a qualified advisor regarding your individual circumstances to learn more on strategies that may be appropriate for you. All examples are intended for illustrative purposes only, highlight a single possible outcome, and do not guarantee that similar results can be achieved.

INTRODUCTION

"Gaining both Wisdom and Wealth in life are worthy goals. Wealth often does not lead to wisdom. Wisdom more often leads to wealth. Wisdom is permanent; Wealth is temporal. So which one is your primary aim?"[1]

—PETER BRANDT

In this book, I will guide you through the wisdom needed to generate and preserve wealth. By the end, you will have seen the path of the most successful investors. The wisdom is hidden in plain sight, but as Henry David Thoreau said, "It's not what you look at that matters, it's what you see." What you *don't* see is costing you the wealth you want. The Best Investors have already shown the way.

---

1   Peter Brandt, Twitter post, April 2020, 11:33 a.m., https://twitter.com/search?q=%22Wealth%20 often%20does%20not%20lead%20to%20wisdom%22%20(from%3Apeterlbrandt)%20 until%3A2020-04-30%20since%3A2020-04-01&src=typed_query.

Whether your investment journey has just begun or you have decades of experience, it is all too easy to fall into believing commonly quoted and overly simplistic assumptions about investing. However, the crucial complexity of markets lies beyond unsubstantiated myths and mantras. The wisdom and experience of the great investment practitioners—our Best Investors—addresses market reality, exposes confused thinking, and reveals a clearer and surprisingly simple structure that can be easily understood and adopted.

In life and investing, I have found that the best way to evolve starts with finding out who is best at what they do, understand it, and then incorporate it into your own process.

Investing is all about numbers, so it isn't hard to identify the few who qualify to be called "Best Investors." This group includes Ray Dalio, Seth Klarman, Stan Druckenmiller, Jim Simons, and others whose insights inform my own investment process and this book. **The secrets, though, lie beyond just the numbers they have achieved over decades. For deep insight into how they achieved durable success, you also need to look at their journeys, discoveries, and choices—and what they all have in common.**

Doing so will focus your investment process and remove the mystery from the big investing questions that come up all the time, which this book will address. So, here are some questions I will ask again at the end of the journey to *Invest Like the Best*. At the end of this book, I believe that most investors will consider them in a new light.

THE BIG INVESTMENT QUESTIONS
RISK AND RETURN

1. Does higher risk lead to higher return?
2. Do you need more than just a return to measure whether your investment process is aligned with the Best Investors?
3. What part has risk and luck played in your return, and what part will they likely play in the future?

MEASUREMENT

1. What are the best-practice measurements of your investment process and progress?

DECISION-MAKING

1. How far from optimal is your own investment thinking and decision process?
2. In investing, do you need to take charge of your own best interest? Can that be made simple?

OTHER STRATEGIC ELEMENTS

1. Do you see rules-based or systematic computer-driven investing as a useful addition?
2. Is passive investing aligned with the Best Investors?

The goal of this book is not to criticize other professionals. Still, you need to know that many financial advisors, famous investors, and so-called experts are not aligned with the Best Investors on the answers to these essential questions. At the end of this journey, though, you will be. You'll gain the clear metrics and understanding that sets apart the few Best Investors from everyone else.

That's why I wrote this book: to empower you. Whether you choose to manage your own assets or work with an investment manager, I want to give you the tools to enable you to stay on the path to prosperity. I particularly want to keep you out of trouble, so you don't learn your investment lessons the hard way and waste crucial time. To succeed, you need more than hope, unsubstantiated beliefs, and insufficient due diligence. You need to know what *works* and *why*.

In my nearly forty years as an analyst, trader, and investor, I have written a book published by Credit Suisse First Boston, been promoted to Managing Director on the proprietary trading desk of JPMorgan in London, and talked to many institutional as well as retail investors. I have worked through many common pitfalls, habits, and beliefs that can misdirect or block unwary investors. This book will give you a productive framework to avoid them all.

The book is laid out in three parts, each with four chapters, and each chapter ends in a summary. (If you want just a quick take, you can start with that summary.) The chapters themselves are filled with quotes and direct advice from the Best Investors; I've also distilled the main takeaways in Part I and Part II as "**Best Investors Insights**" so that you can easily review them. All twenty-four insights are listed in an appendix at the end of the book. In the chapters, I've included charts, visuals, and graphics to better explain my points, as well as additional resources you can look at to deepen your knowledge.

The intention is to make the journey to "invest like the best" as accessible as possible.

Here's a roadmap of what's to come:

PART I: DEVELOP A BEST INVESTORS MINDSET
As the Best Investors show us, durable advantage comes from developing an optimal mindset.

CHAPTER 1: BE FULLY AWARE OF THE INVESTMENT CHALLENGE
With a quick look at our discretionary biases, this chapter shows us how to be grounded in the importance of responsibility, understand the lim-

itations of focusing solely on returns, embrace uncertainty, and realize how many cognitive biases can influence your decision-making process.

CHAPTER 2: AVOID SELF-SABOTAGE: BUILD AN INVESTMENT MINDSET FRAMEWORK

Here, a Best Investor mindset framework is developed. It starts with the key question of whether our own thinking is consistently rational. Investors can benefit from understanding the perspective of different economic approaches and the difference between theory and practice. This leads on to how the hardwiring of the brain reveals a framework to improve decision-making.

CHAPTER 3: BENEFIT FROM SYSTEMATIC INVESTING

Rational and strategic thinking can be strongly supported and further developed by systematic investing. Specifically, two systems reveal how this can extend and transform your capabilities.

CHAPTER 4: AVOID MISDIRECTION: WHAT CAN HAPPEN IF YOU JUST CHASE RETURNS

The final stage in creating an optimal mindset is learning who and what to trust. Through lessons from the collapse of one of the world's biggest hedge funds, LTCM, several filters emerge and reveal what needs to be done to protect your capital.

PART II: RISK AND RETURN, DYNAMIC COMPOUNDING, AND ASSESSMENT

With the optimal mindset now established from Part I, Best Investor practices are explained and revealed. Best Investors are crystal clear about investment principles and metrics. This leads to a further transformation in investment perspectives and strategic thinking and assessment.

CHAPTER 5: BEST INVESTORS ARE CRYSTAL CLEAR ABOUT PRIORITIES AND METRICS

This chapter will explore how Best Investor metrics flow directly from basic concepts of expected return and breaking down return into its more important components. In general, this differs from the approach of most financial advisors.

CHAPTER 6: MASTER THE ESSENTIAL MATH OF INVESTING: DYNAMIC COMPOUND INTEREST

A clear understanding of the dynamics of compound interest is essential and reinforces the Best Investor imperative of how capital preservation and compounding work together in producing high long-term returns.

CHAPTER 7: EMPOWER YOURSELF THROUGH MEASUREMENT

Now, it becomes clearer how to look at allocation and investment choices: through Best Investor metrics. How your performance is reported is vital to your understanding of whether you are on track. All you need is a simple chart. This immediately shows you where you stand and what track you are on.

CHAPTER 8: KNOW THE INVESTMENT MYTHS AND HERESIES WITH BEST INVESTOR ANALYSIS

With the Best Investor metrics in place, common strategies can be reexamined through a new lens. With our newfound knowledge, standard strategies begin to look like myths, while heresies start to make more sense.

PART III: INVEST LIKE THE BEST

The hard work of the first two parts is rewarded as the metrics are put into practice in investment decisions. This final part explores and develops the low-risk road to high returns.

CHAPTER 9: MONEY MANAGEMENT MATTERS

This chapter shows how just taking publicly available billionaire positions and applying Best Investor principles in money management can help lead to remarkable transformations in results.

CHAPTER 10: INVESTMENT ALLOCATION

Building on this theme, we'll explore other low-risk methodologies and optimal allocation choices that improve results.

CHAPTER 11: ACTIVE INVESTMENT MANAGEMENT

This chapter will examine the necessity of active management and how it works with cycle systems.

CHAPTER 12: DECISIVE COMPREHENSIVE PROCEDURE FOR CONSISTENT PERFORMANCE

We'll show how multiple models and research insights operating together can deliver procedural and repeatable Best Investor results.

Investing like the best can lower your stress and risk levels while bringing you higher, long-term returns. It can provide a stable platform for planning and give you more financial security now and for the rest of your life. Let's get started.

PART I

DEVELOP A BEST INVESTORS MINDSET

"True wisdom comes to each of us when we realize how little we understand about life, ourselves, and the world around us."

—SOCRATES

"Humility is not about having a low self-image or poor self-esteem. Humility is about self-awareness."

—ERWIN RAPHAEL MCMANUS

To truly invest like the best, it's important to begin by addressing foundational issues that need to be set straight at the outset. Investors usually ignore these mindset issues; Best Investors never do. Remember, you may be smart and successful in many ways—after all, you've accumulated capital to invest—but investing is unlike anything else. A positive attitude is great, but even with extensive experience, there is always much to learn.

In this part, we'll explore those foundational issues that need to be set right, how to develop a Best Investor mindset framework to avoid self-sabotage, how systematic investing can help, and finally, how to avoid misdirection.

Ray Dalio, a fifty-year veteran Investment Manager of one of the world's biggest hedge funds, wrote in his recent book:

"I'm a 'dumb shit' who doesn't know much relative to what I need to know."

Humility and awareness are where the book starts. If you don't check out your own mindset, this could block your ability to stay on the path to investing like the best. If Ray Dalio constantly reviews his own investment mindset, then, most likely, you should too.

CHAPTER 1

BE FULLY AWARE OF THE INVESTMENT CHALLENGE

"The biggest investing errors come not from factors that are informational or analytical, but from those that are psychological."

—HOWARD MARKS

"The investor's chief problem—and his worst enemy—is likely to be himself. In the end, how your investments behave is much less important than how you behave."

—BENJAMIN GRAHAM (WARREN BUFFETT'S
TEACHER AND MENTOR)

The quotes from Howard Marks and Benjamin Graham show where to start the journey to invest like the best. In their view, by far, the most important part of investment success has nothing to do with economics, asset selection, or portfolio analysis. It has to do with you. Unless you begin by addressing the behavioral and psychological issues that form your investment mindset, you could be headed on a suboptimal or even fatally flawed path.

How you behave and think about investing matters. Your financial future will flow from there. Before you take the first step into investing—or next step if you've invested before—make sure you are confident that you understand the landscape and how to navigate it. This is not an easy task. This is a fast-moving, nonlinear, multidimensional arena over which you have no control—simply hiring financial advisors and an investment team is not enough. There is no guarantee they make the grade of Best Investor. You need to know what that is first.

It's important that you stay informed, that you have the best sources and information to support you, and that you have a clear and effective investment philosophy. But that can be a daunting task. Where do you begin? What information do you need? How will you address whatever could happen in this uncertain and dynamic arena?

The best way to start your journey to investing like the best is to *listen* to the best. Watch what the Best Investors do. Learn from their experiences. Consider the specific challenges they had to overcome to achieve their success, and always consider how to be like them. This will help you develop a Best Investor *mindset*—and that's important because successful investing often runs contrary to human nature. To truly follow in the Best Investors' footsteps, you'll need to check some of your own impulses, intuitions, and thought processes. In short, you'll need to evaluate your own behavior and make behavior adjustments, which can be challenging.

This book is here to help. Through "Best Investors Insights" in this chapter, we'll touch upon the main cornerstones of this mindset that need your direct attention. Even if you've been investing for years or even decades, it's important to review and stay grounded with the basics. Challenge your own investment beliefs and rethink everything to let in the full wisdom of the Best Investors. This leads to a far more effective set of priorities and assessments. And *that's* the key to transforming your investment prospects.

Let's look at some areas that may need your direct attention.

RESPONSIBILITY

Best Investors Insight 1: Take full responsibility for everything.

If you choose an investment manager, take full responsibility for that choice. Did you choose well, and are you sufficiently monitoring the manager and using the right tools and assessments?

On the other hand, if you manage your own account and you're surprised by a sudden loss, do you blame someone or something else for what you believe contributed to the loss? Or do you accept that the losing position included some risk? Do you then check whether that risk was allocated appropriately and whether the trading plan includes what to do next? The latter response will help you learn from the experience and do better next time.

Unless you accept responsibility for all of your decisions, you can't learn and improve. You're setting yourself up for painful lessons down the road and crucial lost time.

RETURNS

Best Investors Insight 2: Don't focus solely on returns.

Investing is complex and requires careful attention and analysis. From the start, you'll need to set your investment objectives to measure your performance accurately. Make sure you're looking at more than just the return.

Return tells you whether you've gotten richer or poorer, and by how much. That is important, but it does not tell you whether you were lucky or skillful, high- or low-risk, or whether you have hit on a strategy worth repeating.

For example, if you doubled your money because you

bought a biotech stock just before the company announced a positive FDA trial result, was that skill? Or was it dumb luck resulting from an inappropriate risk? All you know is that this time, it worked out in your favor, but not whether you are going to be rich or poor over time if you repeat the investment process. A huge gain is great, but it also reflects a high risk. If the event had gone the other way, the *loss* would likely also have been huge. Too many losing trades could wipe out your capital.

What matters is *how you assess* the skill of the process, not just measure the return. An investor controls only the investment *process*, not the outcomes of individual trades. Only looking at returns, and, particularly, shorter-term returns, not only tells you very little about the skill of the process, but it can also be misleading. It may reflect high risk and luck, rather than a durable and skillful process.

Instead of focusing on returns alone, measure your process to understand how you achieved your results.

DON'T CHASE THE PAST

Many investors are drawn to past high returns like a moth to light. But those past returns don't simply translate into great future returns. If anything, they typically lead to buying high and selling low. Most studies show that "chasing returns," as it's called, is a poor allocation strategy.

Applied appropriately and combined with other factors, momentum can be valuable, but it doesn't usually work well alone.

For example, the table[2] below examines data over a sixty-year period. It shows that after WWII, investors consistently increased allocation, or the percentage of their assets invested, in line with how high the prior ten-year returns were. Using returns as their primary assessment metric, they chased good past performance. It follows that allocations peak just as subsequent returns reach their lowest point.

Thus, as you can see in the data below the chart, "Average household stock allocation" reached 54.7 percent in the highest quintile. But this peak allocation level came with the lowest average return of all the quintiles of just 4.1 percent over the next ten years. The reverse was the case for the lowest quintile of "Average household stock allocation" of 28.9 percent. This smaller group achieved a much higher return of 16.4 percent on average, almost four times as much!

---

2   See Liz Ann Sonders, Twitter post, December 26, 2019, 10:41pm, https://twitter.com/LizAnnSonders/status/1206622958640357379.

Household stock allocation (left)

Subsequent S&P 500 rolling 10-year total returns (right-inverted)

Household stock allocation quintile	Average household stock allocation	S&P 500 total return (10-years later)		
		Low return	High return	Average return
Highest 20%	54.7%	-3.0%	8.4%	4.1%
2nd highest 20%	50.1%	0.4%	10.9%	6.9%
3rd highest 20%	45.8%	5.5%	16.4%	10.4%
4th highest 20%	36.3%	8.5%	18.1%	13.3%
Lowest 20%	28.9%	13.7%	19.4%	16.4%

Too much focus on return does not seem to pay off even for the highest-paid professional investors. Those are hedge funds, whose fees and rewards are so closely linked with their return performance that it is hard for them *not* to prioritize returns. In the first half of 2020, hedge funds, in general, failed to provide an acceptable alternative in volatile conditions, losing 7.9 percent over this period[3] just when they are supposed to do relatively well.

To drive your optimal investment process and better assess your performance, you now know you need to do more than just focus on returns.

3   Daniela Sirtori-Cortina, "Hedge funds lost a record 7.9% in pandemic-plagued first half," *Bloomberg*, July 8, 2020, https://www.bloomberg.com/news/articles/2020-07-08/ hedge-funds-fell-a-record-7-9-in-pandemic-plagued-first-half.

PREDICTING THE FUTURE

Best Investors Insight 3: Don't assume you can know the future.

Commit to thinking about the future by making decisions only through the lenses of humility and probability.

"I asked thousands of people to play a simulated stock market game, under time pressure...and what I found was that, over and over, people would overestimate the control they had over events...The more they overestimated their own skill relative to luck...the less they learned from what the environment was trying to tell them."

—MARIA KONNIKOVA, *THE BIGGEST BLUFF*

Many people seem to believe that they know what the future will bring. It's fine to talk about what *could* happen, but no investment allocation or strategy should become anchored to any one outcome.

Beliefs are pervasive, powerful, and part of who we are. They influence investment mindsets, whether consciously or subconsciously. Be aware that if you carry the wrong baggage on your investment journey, you'll pay the price. What works well in professional or social situations could be a behavioral disadvantage in your investing. Strong beliefs, forecasts, or assumptions of knowledge can anchor you into a flawed conviction about outcomes. Accept that you are not in control of the environment, only yourself.

Another pitfall involving a too-narrow focus is letting your ego tell you that you're "right" about the market or a decision. No one decision should matter that much. It's a problem with your strategy if it does. The markets don't care if you are right or wrong; you will be both—and frequently—and it proves nothing.

"It's not whether you're right or wrong, but how much money you make when you're right and how much you lose when you're wrong."

—GEORGE SOROS

The Best Investors plan for any outcome, and they execute on those plans. They focus on their process and know it will involve gains and losses. Best Investors are like casino managers, who understand the odds are in their favor over time, rather than the gamblers who believe they can spectacularly beat the odds and make a fortune. Those gamblers are like investors who have become committed to a single outcome. They have stopped assessing conditions, so they are not ready for alternative action if it becomes necessary. They are setting themselves up for suboptimal investing and possibly significant loss.

COGNITIVE BIASES

Best Investors Insight 4: Be aware of the ways in which your own investment process may be falling short.

The number of known cognitive biases is just an indication of how extensive this issue is.

"In study after study, people fail to internalize numeric rules, making decisions based on 'gut feelings' and 'intuition' and 'what feels right,' rather than based on the data they are shown."

—MARIA KONNIKOVA, *THE BIGGEST BLUFF*

We've highlighted a few key investment mindset issues in the sections above, but these only scratch the surface when it comes to cognitive biases and the investment pitfalls they can lead you to. To get a sense of this subject's scope, you can check out a detailed infographic at Visual Capitalist.[4] It shows a full list of known cognitive biases, all of which may play a part in your decisions and negatively affect your investment strategy.

SUMMARY

The Best Investors make it clear that mindset is where investing really begins. These first steps on your investing journey are very important to get right; facing up to yourself, being aware, and understanding key issues is essential if your journey is going to be successful. This chapter has explored key areas that need your direct attention at the

---

4   Jeff Desjardins, "Every single cognitive bias in one infographic," Visual Capitalist, September 25, 2017, https://www.visualcapitalist.com/every-single-cognitive-bias/.

outset—basic principles that establish a strong foundation for a good investment mindset.

- Best Investors Insight 1: Take full responsibility for everything.
- Best Investors Insight 2: Don't focus solely on returns.
- Best Investors Insight 3: Don't assume you can know the future. Commit to thinking about the future by making decisions only through the lenses of humility and probability.
- Best Investors Insight 4: Be aware of the ways in which your own investment process may be falling short. The extent of known cognitive biases is just an indication of how extensive this issue is.

Now that we're grounded in the issue of mindset and have started to focus on building a better foundation, let's look at establishing a full investment mindset framework.

CHAPTER 2

AVOID SELF-SABOTAGE: BUILD AN INVESTMENT MINDSET FRAMEWORK

"To invest successfully, one doesn't need a stratospheric IQ. What's needed is a sound intellectual framework for making decisions and the ability to keep emotions from corroding that framework."

—WARREN BUFFETT

"But investing isn't about beating others at their game. It's about controlling yourself at your own game."

—BENJAMIN GRAHAM

Sure, it's exciting to talk about big market moves, speculative and volatile stocks, and great wins. Investors do it all the time. But the Best Investors realize that nothing is more important than their own investment mindset. Perhaps this is less engaging in social conversation, but it is what matters most over time for an investor.

The mindset landscape extends beyond what has already been discussed to economics and brain function. These two parts are closely related but play different roles in the investment decision process. One focuses mainly on how we process external information; the second focuses more on our individual internal process. Both need a grounded framework to provide clarity and direction at the outset.

Economics is the starting point, as it best describes the mindset evolution, and it serves a double purpose as the economic discussion will also provide a basis for how economics plays a part in the investment decision process later in this book. This comes into view specifically in chapters 3, 6, 8, and 11.

The extent of available data for investment decision-making can be overwhelming, and even then, it needs to be filtered down into a manageable and productive format for decision-making. Some key distinctions have already emerged from the history of economic thought. An understanding of how this evolved shows the path to a productive Best Investor economic mindset framework.

This economic discussion also leads us to the Best Investor internal investment mindset framework.

An effective framework must sufficiently and accurately address complexity and provide guidance on developing and *practicing* your mindset. Only once this is set are you ready for the next steps.

Over time, through trial and error, experience, and perseverance, good practitioners will always find out what actually works. What practitioners use and what theories are academically acceptable are not necessarily compatible. It has been this way in economics for over a hundred years. Best Investors are practitioners first and foremost.

Our short discussion on economics will lead to behavioral economics, brain function, and then into our investment mindset framework. This is a crucial and foundational part of the journey because at its source lies an unavoidable question at the core of the decision process. So, it requires examination, understanding, and resolution.

Are our own minds rational or irrational, even if they are irrational in predictable ways?

"CLASSICAL" OR "BEHAVIORAL" ECONOMICS?

Extensive economic work over recent centuries, commonly called **classical economics,** makes a major assumption— that **the "economic man"** always acts rationally. This means that economists can, therefore, develop assumptions about how people will act, eliminating choice in their models.

At a deeper level, I believe this strain of economics is constantly attempting to turn economic issues into solvable mathematical problems and solutions. The great issue with this approach is whether the subject matter and assumptions realistically translate to and from an economist's mathematical formula.

In more recent times, **behavioral economics** has become a growing alternative approach. Here is a definition described when a Nobel Prize was awarded to a behavioral economist:[5]

> "Unlike the field of classical economics, in which decision-making is entirely based on cold-headed logic, behavioral economics allows for irrational behavior and attempts to understand why this may be the case. The concept can be applied in miniature to individual situations, or more broadly to encompass the wider actions of a society or trends in financial markets."

In academic circles, this assumption about the rational economic man has, in general, dominated over the last few

---

5   Richard Partington, "What is behavioural economics?" *The Guardian*, October 9, 2017, https://www.theguardian.com/world/2017/oct/09/what-is-behavioural-economics-richard-thaler-nobel-prize.

centuries. Nevertheless, this perspective has constantly run into limitations. Over the last three hundred years, there have been many great insights that have signaled what could be missing from classical economic orthodoxy.

As far back as the eighteenth century, David Hume appeared to believe more in behavioral economics. Hume was an opponent of "philosophical rationalists." He held that passions rather than reason govern human behavior, famously proclaiming that "Reason is, and ought only to be, the slave of the passions."

Hume seemed to believe that our minds can be ingenious at creating a rationale for doing what our emotions have already decided we want to do. Rationale is very different from rational, objective reasoning. While our brain can do both, it is often far from clear—particularly to ourselves—which is which! For investing decisions, this really matters.

Adam Smith's "invisible hand" perspective—which proposed that a free market would, in due course and naturally, fulfill society's needs and act in its benefit—was not far off from the eventual breakthrough but was not examined in sufficient detail. However, one of the great failings of the "classical" economists was that they believed that, based on their sweeping assumptions, market prices could be calculated from one of their formulas. Their inability to satisfactorily solve their equations left them in a quandary that they termed the "Paradox of Value," which was really an admission of failure on this issue. In an article titled "Biography of Carl Menger: The Founder of the Austrian School (1840-1921)," Joseph T. Salerno highlights this main failing:[6]

> "Unable to ground their price theory in the subjective values of consumers, the Classical economists turned to objective costs of production to solidify their theoretical system."

The full article is an excellent examination of the core differences between these two economic approaches. It also describes Carl Menger's profound economic breakthrough in *Principles of Economics*, published in 1871, which explains a universal system of price determination that still stands up today. It essentially rests on just two words in the quote above: "subjective values."

"Subjective" is a refutation of the rational economic man. It means that every individual actor has their own perspective, leading to different choices and actions. Any a priori assumption that human action can be predetermined and is predictable is questionable at best.

"Values" means that there are many different actors and

---

6   Joseph T. Salerno, "Biography of Carl Menger: The Founder of the Austrian School (1840-1921)," Mises Institute, August 8, 2020, https://mises.org/library/biography-carl-menger-founder-austrian-school-1840-1921.

choices, they change over time, and these all contribute to price determination. Consumers and producers are constantly adapting and interacting to price, and so this is a dynamic process. In other words, it is complex in a way that challenges mathematical definition.

These two words—subjective values—show that Menger embraced both complexity *and* behavioral economics to solve the problem of price determination. Steps that the "classical" economists were unable to execute.

MAKE SURE YOUR ASSUMPTIONS AND THEORIES ARE WELL-GROUNDED.

Best Investors Insight 5: Theory and assumptions can help a great deal in development, but investors need to be grounded in facts, evidence, math, and reality. What works in markets is behavioral economics and embracing complexity.

Menger's powerful insight founded the "Austrian School" of economics, but this way of thinking has remained marginalized by mainstream academic economics. This explains the limitations of so much economic theory and, to a degree, also the shortcomings of economic policy. Complexity and behavioral perspectives are very often ignored or assumed away even to this day. A Socratic approach is a wiser perspective.

Behavioral economics received a further boost in the 1970s, and, in more recent decades, complexity has become more widely researched and, to some degree, accepted.

ACCEPTING IRRATIONALITY

Best Investors Insight 6: Understand and then optimize your brain function.

Human behavior is deeply irrational. The groundbreaking work of Kahneman and Tversky in the 1970s demonstrated the countless ways in which this is true, highlighting the common contradictions embedded in the blueprint of the brain.

Their work is relevant for two reasons:

1. They discovered useful and universal truths about human behavior. The cognitive biases and habits of flawed thinking that all humans have are based on the structure of how the brain works.
2. They debunked the myth of "rational economic man." Knowing that rationality is a myth is important as an investor because the "ghost" of the rational economic man still exists in much of current thinking—so be on guard, as flawed assumptions, policy errors, and misleading conclusions are common and should even be expected!

You cannot move toward consistent, rational investment decisions until you are aware of the issues covered so far, understand the hardwiring of your brain, and use behavior modification. The good news is that you *can* compensate for them all—just by adjusting your own behavior and process.

Before we get to the investment mindset framework, brain function needs to be better understood to learn how to make the optimal adjustments.

THE TWO-SYSTEM BRAIN: INVESTMENT MINDSET FRAMEWORK

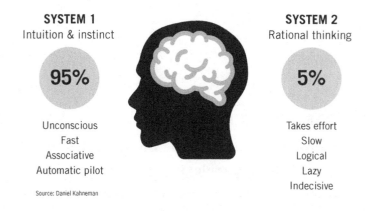

SYSTEM 1		SYSTEM 2
Intuition & instinct		Rational thinking
95%		**5%**
Unconscious		Takes effort
Fast		Slow
Associative		Logical
Automatic pilot		Lazy
		Indecisive

Source: Daniel Kahneman

"You don't literally have two brains. It's not like there's a spare somewhere. But the human brain has two different "systems," which Daniel Kahneman calls System 1 and System 2. To save energy, the built-in preference of the brain—call it the "default setting"—is to use System 1 (fast and intuitive) as much as it can and System 2 (slow and deliberate) as little as it can.

This is the factory-installed set of habits that all brains start out with. (You can change these settings, but only with repetition and the formation of new habits.)

There are two simple ways to help with the problem of "thinking with the wrong brain," or in other words, using System 1 when you're supposed to be using System 2. These two simple things are:

· Developing a clear set of rules, which exist outside your brain, for System 1 to rely on
· Reducing the cognitive expense of System 2 by using software[7]

THE INVESTMENT MINDSET FRAMEWORK

Best Investors Insight 7: The Investment Mindset Framework develops rules to contain System 1 brain functions while adding software systems to boost System 2.

As you develop your investment mindset framework, rely

---

7   See TradeSmith Research Team, "Cognitive bias series #4: The high cost of thinking with the wrong brain," *TradeStops by TradeSmith*, July 31, 2018, https://tradestops.com/blog/cognitive-bias-series-4-high-cost-thinking-wrong-brain/.

on two simple ways to avoid "thinking with the wrong brain." We'll look at each in turn.

1. **Develop a checklist of rules that exist outside your brain for System 1 to rely on.**

This checklist should be based on Best Investor criteria and can help you implement checks on your own cognitive biases. A simple example of one rule on your checklist as an investor is: "limit a loss on any position." One of the best ways to do this is to use trailing stops on every position. What this means is that once a buy trade is initiated, a sell decision can be made simultaneously, so a plan B is automatically in place. The price of an automatic sale can be set so that an acceptable worst-case loss can be determined right from the outset.

By limiting loss, you also minimize the fear response in System 1 of your brain. By calculating and setting boundaries, it also lets System 2's strategy brain relax. It eliminates the immediate need for further thought, and the parameters can be reviewed at any time and with less emotional override.

When returns sag, instead of thinking, *Everything is fine; it will come back; we just need to be patient,* investors who don't have a trailing stop can easily default to this: *I am so consumed by worry about this painful situation, I just want to get rid of it!* That emotional-override response will force selling at a potentially bad time with an out-of-control outcome. Your checklist will help save you from that panicked response and the potential associated losses.

Trailing stops can be a very valuable investment technique, and apart from their risk and return benefits, they provide an example of how investment techniques can also optimize brain function. In chapter 9, this technique will be discussed further.

As you develop your investment process, you can add rules to your checklist, not only for greater profitability but also to minimize the likelihood of negative System 1 interference.

2. **Use software to reduce cognitive expense and boost the effectiveness of your process.**

Using systems software introduces a clearly predefined investment process and optimizes the brain function by reducing System 2's energy drain. A systematic process allows you to take additional steps beyond your set of rules, to ensure rational decision-making and add improvements to your process. It also means it is based on valid, consistent assumptions and can be tested.

Having a software package for investing decisions, though, does not mean that your two-brain systems completely go to sleep! Money is on the line, and you will still react to the results.

Trading a system where complexity goes beyond intuition and understanding can be very hard to sustain when there is any string of losses. It becomes much harder to adjust or reengineer a system you don't fully understand. You'll find that the more the rule checklist and software remain relatively simple, intuitive, and understandable, the more you'll likely benefit. Increasingly, you'll learn to respect the rules and results and how to react to them. Having confidence in your investment process is a key element in effectively executing it.

SUMMARY

· Best Investors Insight 5: Theory and assumptions can help a great deal in development, but investors need to be grounded in facts, evidence, math, and reality. What works in markets is behavioral economics and embracing complexity.

· Best Investors Insight 6: Understand and then optimize your brain function.

· Best Investors Insight 7: The Investment Mindset Framework develops rules to contain System 1 brain function while adding software systems to boost System 2.

In addressing basic economic and behavioral issues,

embracing complexity, and resetting your thinking and awareness, a more productive perspective becomes possible. The investment mindset framework provides a model to optimally enhance your ability to operate effectively. Build your own checklist and introduce systems software to transform your abilities.

Understanding the structure of your investment mindset framework will set you up for constant development, expansion, and improvement. It will allow you to start examining investment options with much greater clarity and direction.

Next, we will examine how investment systems can help the investment process.

CHAPTER 3

BENEFIT FROM SYSTEMATIC INVESTING

"Trying to forecast based upon fundamentals is just opinion. That is not reliable, for we all have good days and bad days. The trend is proven by the analysis."

—MARTIN ARMSTRONG

"If you make money, you feel like a genius—if you lose, you're a dope...It's just too hard to do it that way...I have to do it mathematically."

—JIM SIMONS

Martin Armstrong and Jim Simons, two of the most successful investors of recent decades, preach and practice systematic investing, rather than anyone's interpretation of current "fundamentals." These investors rely on mathematical models—or investment systems—as opposed to "intuition" or "instinct." As Nick Maggiulli notes in his article for *Of Dollars and Data*:[8]

> "Early on, Simons made a decision to dig through mountains of data, employ advanced mathematics, and develop cutting-edge computer models, while others were still relying on intuition, instinct, and old-fashioned research for their predictions. Simons inspired a revolution that has since swept the investing world."

A quick look at the return chart of the Medallion Fund, which Simons runs, corroborates the benefits of this approach:

Annual Returns for the S&P 500 vs. the Medallion Fund (Net of Fees)

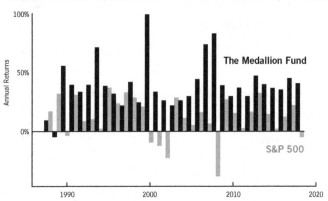

Source: DFA, Grego Zuckerman (OfDollarsAndData.com)
Note: Shows the total annual returns for the S&P 500 and the Medallion Fund (net of fees).

---

8   Nick Maggiulli, "Why the Medallion Fund is the greatest money-making machine of all time," *Of Dollars and Data*, November 19, 2019, https://ofdollarsanddata.com/medallion-fund/.

To bypass flawed discretionary decision-making and improve the investment process, you must build in systemic approaches. Chapters 1 and 2 have shown how flawed our own discretionary decision-making can be and how complex the investment landscape really is. Rationality is not a quality we can take for granted. Investment systems help us overcome these shortcomings. Never underestimate their value: not only do systems help you avoid relying so heavily on your own thinking, they also save you from becoming a victim of someone else's misguided opinion or recommendation.

Who knows how well someone else's advice has been constructed? It may be a relief to pass the burden of research and choice on to someone else, but how will you do the required due diligence? You have no way of knowing how that person formed the opinion, so it needs at least as much analysis and scrutiny as you would bring to your own thinking. It might even need greater effort just to ensure any other party will act in your best interest. By contrast, systems provide clarity, transparency, and objectivity. They are also fully under your control.

Investing involves multiple decisions over a period of years and decades. In practice, without using technology and systems, it is doubtful that optimal execution is even possible. Systematic use of data increases consistency, measurement, and checking. The process is based on facts and math, so it invites testing. Furthermore, the software allows a much greater scope to experiment and find out what matters mathematically. The variety of methodologies for examination, experimentation, and optimization is endless.

Don't be put off if the idea of trading mathematically sounds challenging. It doesn't require a PhD in math (although you may need a guide at first). There is an art to making it work without getting involved in pages of complex mathematical symbols.

For example, here are two accessible and valuable investment systems:

THE SIMPLE TREND SYSTEM

The **Simple Trend System** is aptly named. It takes just one sentence to describe, and it involves no more than high school math, but it's astonishingly effective.

This system has been tested over four decades, including the 1970s—a very different macroeconomic environment from the following three decades. In the 1970s, interest rates typically rose, and the stock market generally traded sideways. Few investment managers can say that they used the same system executed consistently on the same set of rules for over forty years.

Only three main asset classes are considered for this system. They are US Stocks, Treasury Bonds, and Gold.

Here is the system's simple execution rule, with all the results shown and summarized below. The simple moving average is just the average price over the period chosen. So, an uptrend is defined by whether the average three-month price is higher than the average ten-month price.

"Invest equally in whatever is going up (defined as 3 month SMA > 10 month SMA)."[9]

As the results show below, the Simple Trend System outperforms all the other individual asset classes, as well as the simple buy-and-hold allocation. Yet, it just takes around five minutes a month to calculate and execute!

The next chart shows clearly that the Simple Trend System consistently outperforms and has a much smoother and consistent performance than other systems. The full data is below the chart.

---

9   For his article on the Simple Trend System, as well as the data behind the next figure, see: Meb Faber, "Three-Way Model," *Meb Faber Research*, June 16, 2015, https://mebfaber.com/2015/06/16/three-way-model/.

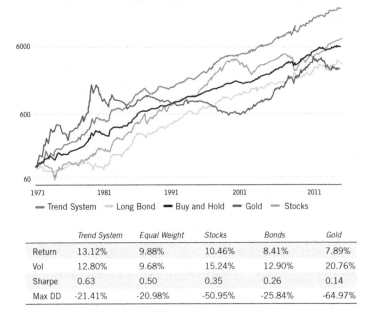

Three Way System

Trend System — Long Bond — Buy and Hold — Gold — Stocks

	Trend System	Equal Weight	Stocks	Bonds	Gold
Return	13.12%	9.88%	10.46%	8.41%	7.89%
Vol	12.80%	9.68%	15.24%	12.90%	20.76%
Sharpe	0.63	0.50	0.35	0.26	0.14
Max DD	-21.41%	-20.98%	-50.95%	-25.84%	-64.97%

The example above shows a significant improvement in long-term return with acceptable metrics, even though the math of the system is extremely simple. Here is a summary:

1. It would just take a few minutes each month to execute.
2. Testing has been possible for forty years.
3. The result shows low risk or at least contained risk, both in terms of volatility and drawdown, the largest correction in an uptrend.
4. The return is higher relative to each of the asset classes alone, and average annualized returns are over 3 percent above an equal weight passive allocation to the

three asset classes combined. Over time, 3 percent a year makes a big difference.

5. In every case, the Sharpe ratio is higher. The Sharpe ratio is one measure of the return relative to the risk taken.

I do not recommend trading this system, as I believe several improvements could be made. Nevertheless, the data makes a clear case that even a simple one-line-of-math system can provide a credible allocation strategy with visible and consistent results. How well would you or an advisor do relative to these results? How much evidence would you be able to go on?

HEDGEYE CYCLE SYSTEM

The **Hedgeye Cycle System** is more involved than the Simple Trend System. If you learn and understand a few concepts, it becomes an accessible and valuable investment aid. It is essentially an institutional level of work and service but is also available in some form to everyone.

The concepts are intuitively easy to understand, and all the data and reports are entirely rules-based. This makes the reports and information completely generated by facts and software and are judgment-free.

It is worth mentioning this system in this chapter because

it shows where systems trading can go and how useful and effective this approach can be. This system is discussed in greater detail in chapter 11. It is relevant here because it can help build on the Simple Trend System above in the three asset classes shown. Very different systems can combine to strengthen their individual effectiveness, a point discussed in chapter 12.

This system also builds on the economic discussion in chapter 2. While economic theory needs to be handled with care, there are many valuable connections between economic data and markets. This relationship just needs a proper understanding and a well-developed practical application to derive effective investment benefits.

As an example, just by using Hedgeye's software system applied to economic data, I was able to see a clear and important market opportunity months in advance.

Hedgeye's high probability predictive algorithm suggested that, after two years of accelerating US growth into the summer of 2018, both growth and inflation would be falling by Q4 2018. If so, asset classes would react in line with multi-decade correlations with economic data. In other words, a major shift from rising growth to declining growth would favor a different portfolio allocation.

Based on Hedgeye's analysis, I wrote and published an

article[10] on June 21, 2018, on the need to shift away from equities in favor of gold and treasuries. Hedgeye's analysis enabled me to clearly see a major portfolio opportunity with plenty of time to position in advance.

The following chart shows that thirty-year Treasury yields reached a two-year peak around three months later, and yields have continued to decline for the following two years as growth has continued to decline. Hedgeye's signal was spot-on.

CBOE 30 Year Treasury Bond Yield Index (INDEX)

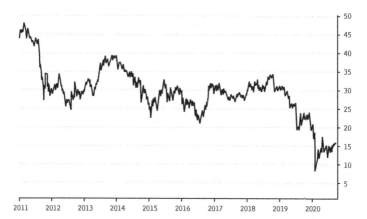

As also indicated, US equities had their worst quarter since 2008 in Q4 2018, as gold and treasuries significantly outperformed. It is now a matter of history that positioning in

10   Chris Belchamber, "Global divergences, challenging cycles, fragile trends, selective allocation," CB Investment Management, June 21, 2018, https://chrisbelchamber.com/global-divergences-challenging-cycles-fragile-trends-selective-allocation/.

favor of gold and treasuries and away from equities was an ideal portfolio structure—but markets only reacted three months after the publication of that article, from October 1, 2018. Hedgeye's system had given a clear signal more than three months in advance. Hedgeye's signal worked out in all three major asset classes.

The Hedgeye Cycle System shows how other systems could add significant value to the first system shown in this chapter.

The leading chart of my July 2, 2020 article[11] shows that this turning point, in the summer of 2018, was also a multi-year turning point in the performance of the S&P 500 Index relative to gold.

EMPOWERING SOFTWARE INVESTMENT SYSTEMS

Best Investors Insight 8: Software investment systems empower you in at least six different ways.

1. —are free of human judgment and decision-making.
2. —can use far more valuable information than anyone could process on their own.

---

11 Chris Belchamber, "Q2 2020 review: Policy chaos adding to economic crisis," CB Investment Management, July 2, 2020, https://chrisbelchamber.com/q2-2020-review-policy-chaos-adding-to-economic-crisis-2/.

3. —allow decisions to be back-tested over multi-decade periods.

4. —can assist with execution signals and portfolio management.

5. —can be used to generate high probability direction of the economy.

6. —can calculate the best allocation for different economic environments.

SUMMARY

Systems investing is so effective that some of the most successful investors use them for all their investment decisions. Two very different systems examples have been explored in this chapter to give you a sense of the benefits of this approach: The Simple Trend System and the Hedgeye Cycle System.

Best Investor's Insight 8: Software Investment Systems empower you in at least six different ways.

When you start to see how usable, effective, and versatile these systems are, you may start to wonder why you need much other investment advice.

In the next chapter, we will examine the history of what was once the world's biggest hedge fund. This case study demonstrates a great deal about the landscape of investing and sets us up for an answer to this essential question: what metrics *must* you measure in real time to determine whether or not you are on the right track?

CHAPTER 4

AVOID MISDIRECTION: WHAT CAN HAPPEN IF YOU JUST CHASE RETURNS

"I'm not so much interested in the return ON my money as I am in the return OF my money."

—WILL ROGERS

"When you want to help people, you tell them the truth. When you want to help yourself, you tell them what they want to hear."

—THOMAS SOWELL

"Risk happens slowly at first, then all at once."

—KEITH MCCULLOUGH

Chapters 1 and 2 showed the questionable investment effectiveness of opinion, whether your own or someone else's.

Then, with our mindset framework in place, chapter 3 introduced systems trading to place more emphasis on strategic, fact-based systematic investing. No opinion even required. Over time it is possible that you won't even need any other advice if you become like Martin Armstrong or Jim Simons, as described in the last chapter.

But for most investors, that outcome is probably years away. In the meantime, you need to know who and what you can trust. Don't minimize the seriousness of wasting time, attention, or money. Avoiding misdirection is vital, whether for research, news, software, or asset management.

This throws up questions of due diligence. Most investors don't do enough to stay on track to "invest like the best," but how can you tell the good advisors from the bad? As we've discussed, just looking at returns is insufficient, so what are the other measures? Who will tell you the truth so you can feel genuinely confident, rather than just comforted by what you want to hear? What is the truth that you need to demand to be sure you are on the right track?

Establishing a clear and effective filter for these choices is essential to becoming a Best Investor. You must know who and what you can trust. Having an effective filter allows you to quickly limit your options to just a few excellent choices and avoid becoming overwhelmed with information and alternatives.

In this chapter, we'll explore the risks of trusting someone else with your money without an effective filter or due diligence in place—as the LTCM story will show, it leaves you open to misdirection. Then we'll discuss what an effective filter looks like and how you can establish it.

LTCM: A CAUTIONARY TALE

What if you found the best possible investment team you could imagine? What if it was run by a famous risk-taker at Salomon Brothers in the 1980s? What if the team included several PhDs, many of whom were Nobel Prize-winning economists and scientists?

And what if the team already had a spectacular three-year track record, with returns greatly surpassing anything else you could find?

Most people would just hand over their money. This is the **Long-Term Capital Management (LTCM)** story. Such was the confidence in this team that LTCM had no problem raising $1.3 billion from the start from many wealthy financial companies and financial professionals. The company's leader was the legendary John Meriwether, who had run the fixed-income arbitrage desk at Salomon Brothers in the 1980s and early 1990s.

What could possibly go wrong?

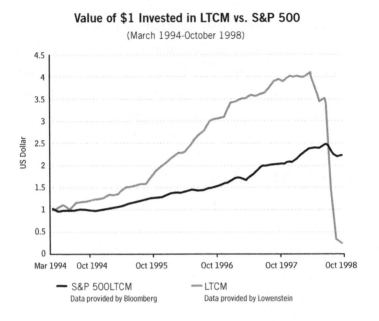

Value of $1 Invested in LTCM vs. S&P 500
(March 1994-October 1998)

US Dollar

| 4.5 |
| 4 |
| 3.5 |
| 3 |
| 2.5 |
| 2 |
| 1.5 |
| 1 |
| 0.5 |
| 0 |

Mar 1994   Oct 1994   Oct 1995   Oct 1996   Oct 1997   Oct 1998

— S&P 500LTCM   — LTCM
Data provided by Bloomberg   Data provided by Lowenstein

As the chart above shows, after a spectacular three-year period, LTCM wiped out in just a few months in 1998. A wipeout is the ultimate failure of investing. Everyone involved lost everything they invested, including the time and energy spent in accumulating that capital.

Given the strength of this management team, though, most investors probably considered that sufficient due diligence had already been done. In addition to the impressive leadership team, the fund showed a good return record during its first three years. Also, the fund's investors, including multiple Wall Street firms, had given it a stamp of approval.

Yet, it's clear in retrospect that something—or many things—was missing from due diligence.

LTCM: WHAT WENT WRONG

The example of LTCM proves why assessing an investment only on returns can lead to tragic outcomes. In the end, the problem was the astonishing risk and leverage adopted by the fund. Here's a clear analysis of what kind of risk LTCM exposed itself to and how it all went wrong.

Best Investors Insight 9: Beware of three types of risk: market, liquidity, and incentive.

MARKET RISK

By all accounts I have seen, the market risks that LTCM was taking had become frankly absurd. In effect, despite all the credentials of the management team and all the trust from all the financial experts invested in the fund, by 1998, LTCM had become an accident waiting to happen.

The positions are described in detail in the links in this chapter. The whole portfolio was twenty-five times the size of the fund's Net Asset Value. That's crazy leverage. This means that just a 4 percent adverse move in the portfolio's value would make the fund insolvent. Yet this was almost nothing compared to the swaps portfolio. Just a 0.4 percent adverse move in the swaps portfolio would also make the fund insolvent.

LIQUIDITY RISK

LTCM's derivatives position represented 5 percent of the entire global market. So, there was also liquidity risk here. It is very likely they could not liquidate a position easily at that level, relative to the size of the market. Indeed, this proved to be a big problem when the fund hit trouble in 1998. This passage was provided by SunGard's BancWare ERisk:[12]

> "Early 1998: The portfolio under LTCM's control amounts to well over $100 billion, while net asset value stands at some $4 billion; its swaps position is valued at some $1.25 trillion notional, equal to 5% of the entire global market. It had become a major supplier of index volatility to investment banks, was active in mortgage-backed securities and was dabbling in emerging markets such as Russia (Risk, October 1998)."

Why would LTCM take risks to levels high enough to threaten the extinction of the fund? Apparently, the managers seemed to believe that historical experience of their positions was acceptable and not a threat. Given the numbers above, that is hard to fathom.

---

12 "Case Study: LTCM," BancWare ERisk by SunGard, Spring 2006, https://www.bauer.uh.edu/rsusmel/7386/ltcm-2.htm.

Best Investors need to do better than be a part of what happened at LTCM. One of them did, by maintaining a *Margin of Safety*—both the title of Seth Klarman's book and his philosophy. When LTCM approached Klarman to buy a stake in the company, he turned them down. Not everyone believed that LTCM's models were so great. In a 2014 article in *Business Insider*, Stephanie Yang writes:[13]

"Seth Klarman, general partner at Baupost Group, had turned down a stake in Long-Term. He believed not accounting for "outlier" events and increasing leverage was incredibly reckless. Any serious mistake on Long-Term's part would wipe out a huge amount of its capital."

There was another liquidity risk in the case of LTCM. Investors in the hedge fund were not allowed their capital back until after three years. That amounts to diminishing your ability to get your money back if the manager does not satisfy you. Remember, managers must earn their right to manage your money every day and remain constantly accountable. You must remain constantly alert to your own best interests. It is unlikely to be in your own best interests to impose limitations on your right to access your capital whenever you want. If you permit this kind of limited access, you have imposed your own liquidity risk on yourself.

---

13   Stephanie Yang, "The epic story of how a 'genius' hedge fund almost caused a global financial meltdown," *Business Insider*, July 11, 2014, https://www.businessinsider.com/the-fall-of-long-term-capital-management-2014-7.

LTCM's provision would have stopped you from any withdrawal even if you had been aware of the excessive leverage and risks LTCM was taking in 1998.

INCENTIVE RISK

It is clear that Meriwether was ambitious about the fee level for LTCM. In the same *Business Insider* article, Stephanie Yang notes:

> "Meriwether had high expectations for his hedge fund that would set it on an entirely different level. First, he wanted to raise capital of $2.5 billion. Second, LTCM's asking fees would be 25 percent of profits on top of an annual two percent charge on assets. Third, investors were required to keep their capital in for a minimum of three years. These standards were incredibly uncommon for a hedge fund to demand."

A related problem is that even if a hedge fund collapses, the consequences can be more severe for the investor than the manager. The manager can move along and start up another hedge fund and begin the whole process over again. John Meriwether went on to start up two more hedge funds. The investor, on the other hand, had lost his savings with no clear path to being able to rebuild what was lost.

Although it seems that most of the partners were also invested in LTCM, it is clear the high fee structure made the managers highly incentivized by the fees to make money on the fund. This may sound like a good approach on the surface, but it actually creates a problematic basis for a strong partnership between investor and manager. These high levels of fees can make managers *too* eager to take risks in the chase for returns and put the investors' capital in danger. Indeed, for the most part, high incentive fees do not appear to have worked out for hedge fund investors over recent decades. As discovered in chapter 1, too much focus on returns seems to be problematic.

The following chart shows evidence that the highest-paid trading experts—hedge funds—who are most incentivized to produce high returns have failed to do so.[14]

---

14 For more information, see Simon A. Lack, "Hedge funds: Still fleecing investors with expensive mediocrity," SL Advisors, https://sl-advisors.com/hedge-funds-high-fees-low-returns-2?print=print.

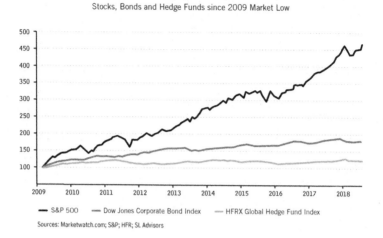

Hedge Funds Generate Fees and Little Else
Stocks, Bonds and Hedge Funds since 2009 Market Low

— S&P 500 — Dow Jones Corporate Bond Index — HFRX Global Hedge Fund Index

Sources: Marketwatch.com; S&P; HFR; SL Advisors

It seems that chasing returns doesn't tend to work even for highly paid professionals, not only for most investors. Again, this is further confirmation that not only is return a poor sole assessment measure, but it is also a very poor primary focus.

I was interviewed by John Meriwether in 1997 for a senior role at LTCM, right near the peak of their reputation. LTCM's European head, Victor Haghani, had sat with me for a day on JPMorgan's proprietary trading desk in London and had invited me back to LTCM's Mayfair office. To my surprise, John Meriwether walked in and introduced himself. We talked about investing and the difference between what we did, and it was a fascinating conversation. The energy in our conversation seemed to slip when we talked about risk.

I have always had issues with the incentives of hedge funds. Charlie Munger is right about this:

"Show me the incentive and I will show you the outcome."

The passage of time has continued to reinforce that perspective. For hedge funds, payday is usually heavily linked to short-term returns, so there is always the risk that short-term returns become the main focus at the cost of risk assessment and appropriate management for compounding long-term returns.

There were clearly multiple issues with risk assessment at LTCM. Could investors have recognized the problem? Yes, given the right information, as Seth Klarman did.

TRUSTING YOUR ADVISORS: EFFECTIVE FILTERS FOR SUCCESS

LTCM is a cautionary tale. Several major conclusions come out of this:

Best Investors Insight 10: Experience and track record are valuable initial requirements but insufficient without clearer metrics and ongoing, real-time measurement.

The experience of the management team and the size of returns are not exceptions.

Best Investors Insight 11: Even at the highest levels of investment management and across the whole financial industry, there is a pervasive intellectual and/or behavioral confusion about the balance between risk and return, both for accurate assessment and for setting investment objectives.

Bearing these conclusions in mind, it's necessary to do your due diligence when it comes to financial advisors or to whomever you ask to invest your capital. It's important for you to understand their incentives and business practices—otherwise, how can you trust them?

Best Investors Insight 12: Be aware of all conflicts of interest.

Here are some issues you should clarify:

1. Investment managers are often paid according to the amount invested in an account and the time it is invested. These managers are better compensated the longer the client's assets stay invested. Passive investing (and restricted withdrawal of capital) is therefore in the manager's best interest, so at the very least, it's a conflict of interest. As the managers derive a bene-

fit from passive investing, they should be required to present evidence of the objective benefit of the passive investment strategy to the investor.

2. Passive investing does not require much time or attention from the manager. All that is needed from time to time, perhaps four times a year, is rebalancing. The only required "skill" is portfolio selection, which may not even be the manager's choice as the manager's firm may have predetermined it. You can determine a manager's skill only by looking at their own account and performance for a minimum of three years. Chapter 8 will examine the issues of passive investing.

3. Be aware of paying double investment fees. If your manager charges an advisory fee for investing in mutual funds that also have additional fees, you are paying fees twice. I have even seen a fee to select a mutual fund that invests in mutual funds, so you can pay fees three times over. Furthermore, why would you take advice from an advisor who does not do the investing directly themselves? Check their direct visible track record or any clear evidence that the advice has clear value.

4. Conflict of interest is one of Wall Street's biggest issues. Most firms receive fees for some securities both on the buy-side and the sell-side. Large firms have massive amounts of information, but which clients get the information and when? Focus instead on research from companies whose only source of income is the fees for their research.

Both the investment managers and their investors need a clear set of rules for monitoring objectives and assessments. These rules don't need to be complicated, but they do need to be transparent and shared for this partnership to work well. From the LTCM example, it should be clear that the onus is on you to demand it.

SUMMARY

- Best Investors Insight 9: Beware of three types of risk: market, liquidity, and incentive.
- Best Investors Insight 10: Experience and track record are valuable initial requirements but insufficient without clearer metrics and ongoing, real-time measurement. The experience of the management team and the size of returns are not exceptions.
- Best Investors Insight 11: Even at the highest levels of investment management and across the whole financial industry, there is a pervasive intellectual and/or behavioral confusion about the balance between risk and return, both for accurate assessment and for setting investment objectives.
- Best Investors Insight 12: Be aware of all conflicts of interest.

To avoid problems of misdirection, develop an effective filter to reduce your choices to a few excellent ones. The history of LTCM, once the world's biggest hedge funds, clearly illustrates that the burden of due diligence falls on you, the investor.

You need to know what metrics to demand from your manager for a better partnership. They need to report far more than just return. You also need to understand the incentives of your counterparties.

You need protection from the kind of disastrous outcomes that few of the financial experts inside or outside of LTCM saw coming. To make sure your own best interests are being served, you need to take charge of your own due diligence.

In Part II, we will go deeper into risk and return concepts and priorities, investment metrics, and ongoing assessments. It will empower you to understand what tools you need, how to apply and measure them, and how to know when to make significant changes.

From this new vantage point, investing will look different. Popular strategies may begin to look unsatisfactory. Other strategies you may not have considered before may work better than you realized. Get ready for a transformation.

RISK AND RETURN, DYNAMIC COMPOUNDING, AND ASSESSMENT

"'Modern' financial theory is founded on a few, shaky myths that lead us to underestimate the real risk of financial markets."

—BENOIT MANDELBROT AND RICHARD L.
HUDSON, *THE (MIS)BEHAVIOR OF MARKETS*

In Part I, the focus was on establishing healthy investment foundations. With a Best Investor mindset framework, an introduction to systems investing, and a good understanding and awareness of other common pitfalls, the stage is set to address the core component of investing—risk and return.

Part II will delve deeper into Best Investor concepts and principles so that you are crystal clear about your investment priorities and know the necessary metrics and tools to evaluate them.

Best Investors Insight 13: The only way investors can feel confident that they are on the path to multi-decade investment success is to adopt and then demand the right priorities and assessments.

Getting clarity on your objectives and assessments provides enormous benefits for investors. The result is nothing less than a material and consequential investment transformation and the safety, stability, and peace of mind that goes with it.

Here is what we'll cover in Part II:

1. The major differences in investment approach between the practices of the Best Investors and the general investment advice given by financial advisors

2. New metrics and priorities for investors to strengthen their selection filters which also provides a solution to the LTCM problem by generating essential and real-time monitoring tools

3. Explain the crucial importance of understanding the dynamics of compound interest

4. Think through the consequences of a new and different set of assessment metrics

5. Show how reporting Best Investor metrics can be easily done

6. And, finally, expose some established myths about investing and introduce some new heresies

Let's get started!

CHAPTER 5

BEST INVESTORS ARE CRYSTAL CLEAR ABOUT PRIORITIES AND METRICS

"Consideration of risk must never take a backseat to return."

—SETH KLARMAN

"Rule No. 1: Never lose money. Rule No. 2: Never forget Rule No. 1."

—WARREN BUFFETT

Perhaps the clearest distinction between the most successful investors and everyone else is that they are not conflicted in their priorities when it comes to risk and return.

RISK

The quotes from Seth Klarman and Warren Buffett are rigid, relentless, and uncompromising. In just two quotes, the word "never" comes up three times. To outperform over multiple decades, there are some principles that successful investors learn to live by. Their number-one principle and primary focus is examining and assessing risk. This is not negotiable.

RETURN RELATIVE TO RISK

As an investor, you put your money at risk because you believe that there is a good prospect of achieving an attractive return, and the risk of failure is acceptable. It is important to be clear about what drives your willingness to invest.

If there were equal odds of winning or losing, but you made twice as much if you won, you would have a positive expected return from taking the risk. That could be attractive to you if the risk of losing was acceptable. If there were equal odds of winning or losing, but you would lose more than you would gain, then the expected return is negative. Best Investors would not participate. This kind of trade-off will make you bankrupt over time.

Best Investors Insight 14: What should drive investment is expected return and risk management. Risk is the

denominator of return/risk and has more impact on the calculation than return. Best Investors are risk-averse.

For sure, investment advice is not one-size-fits-all. It comes in all shapes and sizes, but when it comes to Best Investors, some principles are set in stone with no room for compromise. Financial advisors' approach is generally very different, and most investors don't realize *how* different.

Most investors are confused about return and risk and the relationship between them. Without clarity, the whole investing venture is exposed to poor decision-making, inappropriate risk, and suboptimal and potentially dangerous portfolio allocation.

TWO INVESTMENT APPROACHES

One of the most important steps in investing is for you to be clear on your investment-management decision process. If you're working with a financial advisor, then it is the responsibility of any advisor to be transparent and clear about their own approach and how it differs from the two standard approaches described below.

To differentiate between these two investment methodologies, two broad investment management approaches are defined and discussed: the one followed by Best Investors and the one followed by financial advisors. (I'm aware there are variations between financial advisors, but for the sake of brevity, I am going to generalize.)

The key difference in methodologies depends crucially on what you believe is the core relationship between risk and return. Is there a simple equation that explains how they interact?

The table below presents the key investment choices in concept, in the simplest form possible, to highlight the basic choices about how to look at different investment approaches.

The expected positive return is derived by comparing the anticipated return relative to perceived risk. There are both high and low levels of risks and returns. So broadly speaking, allocation of capital comes down to four broad categories.

It is remarkable that different investment experts allocate to different parts of this table below:

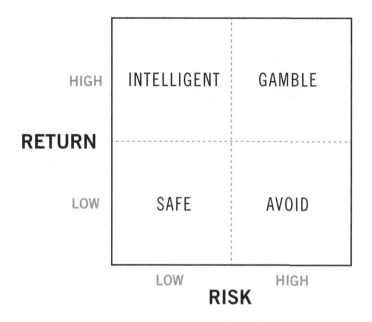

1. **The Best Investors focus exclusively on the left hand "low-risk" side of the table.** Risk is the primary focus. As much as possible, they want "intelligent," high reward for low risk. If they can't find it, they default to "safe" because they have no interest in straying into "gamble" or "avoid."

To simplify, Best Investors take a low-risk approach with a sole focus on high return to risk.

2. **Most financial advisors usually focus as much as possible on the right-hand "high-risk" side of the table.** They subscribe to the view that high risk is the way to make high long-term returns. This is why the

financial industry tests for an investor's capacity to take risk, so they can maximize how much they can allocate to the right-hand "high-risk" side of the table. Essentially, allocation is primarily driven by a risk-level determination according to client "suitability."

Financial advisors will end up allocating to both sides of the risk table to reach a balance that matches the investor's risk level. The portfolio is reviewed periodically, and in the interim, is rebalanced to maintain the portfolio allocation.

These are entirely different sets of approaches.

Investors need to be very clear about these two different standards, as they will lead in radically different directions with very different outcomes.

HOW THE BEST INVESTORS APPROACH WORKS FOR INVESTORS

How Best Investors intend to achieve their results is so clear that it can be described mathematically. In concept, what drives return is the product of risk and (return/risk):

Risk × (Return/Risk) = Return

For Best Investors, the day-to-day focus is on the left-hand side of this key equation and could be better described as:

Low Risk × High (Return/Risk) = High Probability of
High Long-Term Return

Or:

Safe × Intelligent = High Probability of High Long-Term
Return

Best Investors have learned the importance of risk management for high long-term returns, so they always want to limit risk. The only way to do that and produce a high long-term return is to maximize return/risk or alpha.

The true test of a Best Investor is to show they are successful in lowering or containing risk while, at the same time, increasing alpha. Just these two elements are by far the most reliable path to durable and positive long-term returns. They are relatively easy to calculate and report, so they can provide a real-time indication of whether an investor is on track for Best Investor results.

If risk is low and alpha is high, then not only are returns more likely positive, but they are also being produced with the highest probability of continued success! The skill of the investor's process is clearly high.

So, low risk and high alpha are the best real-time and long-term measures of the Best Investors' process. The short-term return provides very little information, but the long-term return will take care of itself in the best possible way if low risk and alpha are being consistently well produced.

Low risk and alpha can also be measured accurately in the short term. They provide much earlier and important insight into the quality and durability of the investment process and the probability of achieving a high long-term return. The short-term return, even after more than three years in the case of LTCM (discussed in chapter 4), tells you almost nothing about the likely long-term return. It may even be completely misleading!

To show this information, calculate the volatility of daily returns, drawdown (which is the biggest temporary loss), and then alpha is readily available. These can be shown for the same period as for the returns you are reporting.

You'll see the key results, and in terms of priority, they are:

1. Risk (volatility of daily returns and drawdown)
2. Return relative to risk
3. Long-term return
4. All of the above compared to a range of benchmarks

Clearly, this permits you to see far more valuable information about process and performance than just return.

The benchmarks provide context for the market conditions during the assessment period for the performance.

This new level of information empowers you and holds the manager far more accountable to you and to what matters most to Best Investors. Now you have a far better measure of the manager's process. You are also able to see whether the manager fits the characteristics of a Best Investor! The process is measurable and within the control of the manager, and much less dependent on risk and luck. This approach will permanently improve the conversation and partnership between you and the manager because it focuses on what you control and what risks you are taking.

THE FINANCIAL ADVISOR APPROACH WITH BEST INVESTOR COMMENTS

There are many unresolved issues with the financial advisors' approach to investment management.

What follows is a description of the financial advisors' approach in black type, with the perspective of the Best Investors written in **bold type** to make clear distinctions between the financial advisors' and Best Investors' investment approaches.

Let's look more closely at financial advisors' tendency to

focus on the right-hand "high-risk" side of the concept table.

1. *There is little clear evidence of a positive correlation between higher risk and higher long-term returns. There is a great deal of evidence that contained intelligent risk is better correlated with higher long-term return. The primary assumption of financial advisors is immediately challenged. Many examples are provided in the rest of this book.*

2. *High risk is prioritized over expected return in allocation decisions. Why? Doesn't this mean that, in concept, "gamble" is preferred to "intelligent"? How could that be justified? "Intelligent" has a higher expected return than "gamble." Why doesn't expected return drive the investment allocation rather than risk?*

Financial advisors do not really look at their approach in the frame of:

Risk × (Return/Risk) = Return

Nevertheless, the logic is undeniable, and the distinctions on the left side of the equation are clearly important and can be calculated and reported for insight.

Financial advisors do not generally believe in active management as they commit to a long-term portfolio allocation.

The risk level of the client is determined in some way and regarded as fixed until the next review. The portfolio has been matched to this risk level and is assumed to be broadly appropriate to the client also until the next review. Return must be reported, but not much will change no matter what market conditions are experienced. The investment approach is, therefore, broadly passive and reactive with a significant delay.

The risk level and the alpha reported won't change how the portfolio is managed, so financial advisors may not see the purpose of reporting them.

1. *A great deal of behavior and complexity has been assumed away. Markets are dynamic and offer constantly changing opportunities and risks. The idea that the only portfolio decision points are at review meetings assumes away the potential importance of taking action in between. The best opportunities and greatest risks in the markets won't wait for the meeting schedule.*

   ○ *In Q1 2020, the VIX, which is a measure of risk or volatility for the S&P 500, varied from around eleven to eighty-five. These are very different market conditions. It is hard to understand how any single portfolio would be optimal throughout this quarter or that no reaction to dramatic changes in market conditions would be necessary during this time.*

2. *The key methodology that "any portfolio can be categorized by a single risk factor" or "any investor can be categorized by a single risk factor" is likely an oversimplification of a higher complex dynamic. Furthermore, these are both assumed to be stable over time. Then there is yet another assumption that they adequately correspond to each other. This requires examination and evidence of effectiveness. These so-called measures and assumptions are also likely to be opinion-based.*

3. *While measuring risk and alpha won't change the allocation process, how can factors that are significant measures of performance efficiency and safety of the investor's capital not be reported? If these are not reported, then the manager is not accountable to these factors even though they are clearly important and in the best interest of investors who want to understand the dynamics and management of the portfolio.*

4. *The recommendation "invest for the long term" is not defined. Furthermore, what evidence is there that the claim "invest for the long term" is beneficial? The major assumption here is that all asset classes will at least recover any loss, or mean revert, within a reasonable time frame. (Some broad analysis of this assumption is shown in chapter 8 and in other parts of this book.)*

Relatively passive approaches can produce strong returns in a bull market largely due to above-average risk levels. However, naturally, the opposite is also the case in a bear market. A successful investment process needs to show that it can produce positive long-term returns through any and all investment environments, and in aggregate, no matter what. *This is not supposed to be a "heads, you win/tails, you lose" experience. Over time, many different investment conditions will be experienced. What assurance is there that this approach will be successful within a reasonable time frame?*

1. *A rigid investment model that ignores market developments for extended periods of time is purposefully not adaptive to either current or even changing investment conditions. This is a simplistic approach, which almost certainly could not be described as optimal by any reasonable definition.*

2. *The Simple Trend System we showed in chapter 3 produced higher returns than any passive allocation approach, with low risk and contained drawdown, and you have over forty years of track record. The clarity and outperformance of this simple system come in sharp contrast to the multiple issues raised by the financial advisors' passive approach. It also challenges the durable merit of any passive approach, given its simplicity, consistency, and outperformance.*

SUMMARY

- Best Investors Insight 13: The only way investors can feel confident that they are on the path to multi-decade investment success is to adopt and then demand the right priorities and assessments.
- Best Investors Insight 14: What should drive investment is expected return and risk management. Risk is the denominator of return/risk and has more impact on this calculation than return. Best Investors are risk-averse.

There are major differences in investment approach between the practices of the Best Investors and the general investment advice of financial advisors. The prerequisites for a Best Investor are low risk and high alpha, which can be measured in real time and measures process and the probability of long-term success. The key metrics empower you and holds the manager appropriately accountable to you.

The next chapter examines an essential and yet widely misunderstood component of investment management—the dynamics of compound interest. This explains why the Best Investors metrics introduced in this chapter work so well. It also examines, in much greater depth, the key relationship between risk and long-term return.

CHAPTER 6

MASTER THE ESSENTIAL MATH OF INVESTING: DYNAMIC COMPOUND INTEREST

Almost everyone thinks compound interest is simple. Instead, dynamic compound interest is complex in a way that will define you as an investor, so make sure you get this right!

"The avoidance of loss is the surest way to ensure a profit-able outcome."

—SETH KLARMAN

"Without capital Preservation, there is no compounding."

—DIEGO PARRILLA

"Rising volatility drives a predictable and emotional response in human beings. It also drives fund flows. Asset allocations flow towards asset classes that have low and falling volatility—they flee those with high and rising volatility."

—KEITH MCCULLOUGH

When it comes to investing, little is more important than understanding the dynamics of risk and return and how to use these two crucial concepts to your best advantage. Risk and return are being addressed appropriately if your returns are compounding positively. Then your account is growing exponentially. They are failing if your returns are not compounding.

Compounded returns are significantly impacted both by losses and also by the variability of returns. Understanding the *dynamics* of compounded returns will help you to determine the line between acceptable and unacceptable results. Simply looking at your return—even if it is spectacular over a three-year period—does not tell you this, as we found out in the LTCM case. LTCM posted high returns for three years, but the high *volatility* experienced by LTCM required attention. Astonishing risk levels, on examination, indicated a "gamble" environment, which no Best Investor would have accepted. Understanding dynamic compound interest could have helped LTCM investors see and understand the risk.

In the real world, your returns will go up and down with varying amplitude and frequency. The next chart shows the power of compounding at a single constant rate. When you are compounding effectively, your returns grow exponentially over the long term. Compounding is where great long-term returns come from.

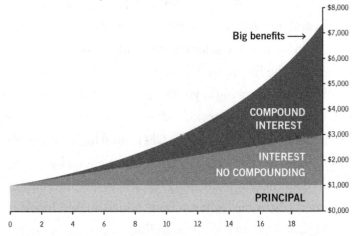

Compound Interest 10% for 20 years

Big benefits ⟶

COMPOUND INTEREST

INTEREST NO COMPOUNDING

PRINCIPAL

What is missing from the chart is that it does not show what happens when returns become *variable* and include losses. Then the *dynamics* of compounding becomes more complicated and, in general, poorly understood.

A deep understanding of dynamic compound interest provides clarity about:

1. How to manage risk and return for optimal long-term results
2. Which conceptual investment approaches make sense
3. How to calibrate your investment decisions
4. What your assessment metrics are telling you in real time about your chances of success

It's important to do the work and ensure that you are grounded in the essential math of investing, so you can stay consistently focused on what is key to accumulating long-term wealth.

RISK AND RETURNS

Before we dive into the math of dynamic compounding, it's necessary to explore common understandings of risk and return and how a simplification of their relationship can lead to a common investing myth: higher risk leads to higher rewards.

In very few human occupations do people embrace risk in isolation of some purpose or prospect of reward. Indeed, even when there is some prospect of reward, it is likely that efforts would be made to mitigate the risks. After all, risk means embracing the possibility of an adverse outcome outside of your control. Who wants that?

Why should investing be any different?

When it comes to investing, however, I find that some people do surprisingly embrace risk as a single factor! It seems that financial advisors believe that, in general, higher risk means higher long-term returns—it's implicit in their standard portfolio advice. It's worth examining that assumption, for which I have yet to see any proof or clear evidence.

Many investors have an equation in mind. If they want high returns, which they do, they believe they need to commit to higher risk. This idea is commonly shown in a diagram like the following chart.

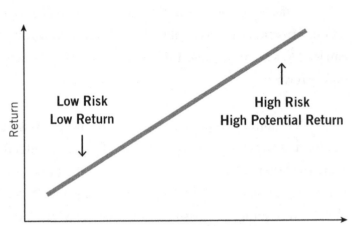

Common Theory Risk / Return Trade-Off

At first sight, this may seem plausible: by definition, the higher-risk asset will move by more than the low-risk asset most of the time. However, all that means is that in a bull market, you probably make greater returns, but in a bear market, you may also lose more. Not a clear result. What really matters is not the volatility but the expected return.

Another point is that most people are dealing with a portfolio of assets, so it is the aggregate return of multiple assets, and not just in a day but over multiple years. All of a sudden, a simplistic idea (however plausible it seems) has become a far more çomplicated puzzle.

Best Investors Insight 15: Best Investors have rejected the widely used theory that higher risk is linked to higher return (as shown in the previous chapter). Finding out more about the evidence and math of your underlying investment assumptions is strongly advised before you invest.

Best Investors Insight 16: Behavioral economics and evidence suggest that higher volatility generally corresponds with FALLING asset prices.

Here is another problem with oversimplifying the relationship between risk and return. In the real world, risk/volatility is not static. In fact, volatility itself is highly volatile. When the behavior of markets is examined, what is observed seems to refute the simple assumption above, just by examining the behavior of individual asset prices with their own levels of volatility. There's a Financial Source[15] video that explains this well; here's a quote from the video:

> "Volatility and asset prices are normally inversely correlated. When volatility increases in a specific market, the value of

---

15 Financial Source, "What is the Correlation between Volatility and Asset Price?" YouTube, April 13, 2020, https://www.youtube.com/watch?v=Yy-1MLmCOvw.

related assets usually falls. When volatility drops off again, the value of assets tends to rise."

Behaviorally, this makes a great deal of intuitive sense. Capital is far less secure to its owner when its value is unstable and changeable. The ability of an investor to plan or rely on their capital for safety is reduced when it is harder to be sure of its value. For a substantial part of anyone's wealth, low volatility is highly desirable.

From this perspective, it's only natural that most investors become less inclined to own any asset, the more volatile it is. The Financial Source video provides evidence that investors run away from assets as volatility rises. The correlation is evident and very clear.

The "high risk/high return" theory above already seems ever more challenged. If behavior and evidence show that rising risk and falling asset prices go together, why would investors then run to higher risk assets? There may be other reasons and situations, but clearly, there is general evidence that the volatility and price trend are often negatively correlated.

It seems that, once again, an overly simplistic assumption has been hardwired into standard investment thinking without being substantiated sufficiently. Even before we start the analysis and math of dynamic compounding, higher risk correlating with high return looks like a stretch!

While this does not end the debate over risk and return, the key point to make at this stage is to be very careful about what assumptions are made in your allocation. Much more analysis is yet to come on this, starting in chapter 8. What can be shown is that Best Investor metrics typically produce a radically different risk to return chart than the one shown above. This is shown in many examples throughout the remainder of this book.

Wouldn't you prefer your higher returns to come with lower risk? This is the path you are now on!

Don't rush into believing anything, no matter how appealing its simplicity may be. Be open and ready to weigh the evidence based on math, facts, and research. Best Investors need more to go on than any untested or unsubstantiated simple concept.

SCARY!

Simple yet essential math moves us away from common investment myths about the relationship between risk and long-term returns.

THE MATH OF DYNAMIC COMPOUNDING

One of the most powerful forces in investing is simply:

CONSISTENTLY COMPOUNDING POSITIVE RETURNS

The following chart shows the exponential account growth assuming 6 percent growth and the importance of time in building your savings.[16]

---

16 For more information, see Andy Kiersz, "Here's the difference between someone who starts saving at 25 vs. someone who starts at 35," *Business Insider*, March 25, 2014, https://www.businessinsider.in/personal-finance/Heres-The-Difference-Between-Someone-Who-Starts-Saving-At-25-Vs-Someone-Who-Starts-At-35/articleshow/32679394.cms.

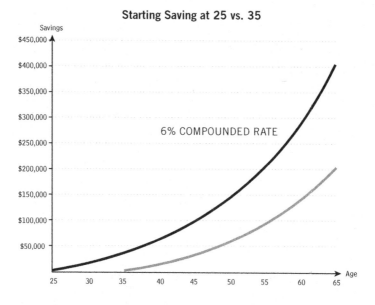

Starting Saving at 25 vs. 35

6% COMPOUNDED RATE

If only it was just that simple! Naturally, the big assumption here is that money can be made consistently at a constant positive rate every year without risk.

Historically, this has sometimes seemed to be a reasonable proxy for the general investment environment. With high enough interest rates, good yields on government bonds, and stable to low inflation, you might get close to those ideal conditions. However, low and sometimes rising interest rates over the last decade mean that the current environment has very different dynamics.

Nevertheless, this is a good start for how to think about the purpose of investing and how compounding consistently positive investment returns can work out very well.

This is what most investors have in mind when they think about investing. What happens in reality when losses are a possibility?

The power of compounding *only works* when you do not lose money.

Once you introduce losses, the whole dynamic changes. Look at the five-year performance of the three managers before you look at the five-year compounded return results that follow it. Can you tell what a difference compounding makes to an investor's long-term performance?

Most investors have far more years than five to invest, so these differences will be far greater over a ten-, twenty-, or even fifty-year period. If you don't understand compounding, you have no idea how to select different managers or even what your chances of success are likely to be.

In the example of the three different manager's returns, which is best?

All the simple interest annual results for each manager below add up to 20 percent over five years, but the compound return is different for all three. Which manager would you choose from the individual five years you saw first? Make your choice before you look at the results on the next page.

Here are 3 different sets of hypothetical returns produced by 3 different asset managers

	Manager A	Manager B	Manager C
Year 1	5%	12%	15%
Year 2	2%	-10%	-40%
Year 3	8%	15%	12%
Year 4	3%	-8%	-5%
Year 5	2%	11%	38%
Added return	20%	20%	20%

Before you turn the page, write down which manager you would choose and why.

Now look at the results below and see whether you were right. Did the difference surprise you? Would you have made a different choice if all you had seen was the last three years?

	Manager A	Manager B	Manager C
Compounded return	21.5%	18.4%	1.3%

This example shows that just looking at a few annual returns is a poor way to make a decision.

These results show the advantage to an investor's long-term wealth of finding a manager with consistently positive returns, even if these returns are all in single digits.

Without outstanding up years, Manager A, at first glance, may seem very uninspiring. However, every year is positive, and despite some small volatility, he is the only manager who experiences a compounded return above the sum of the annual returns, which are the same for each manager.

By contrast, a glance at the last three years of their returns, Manager B and Manager C might look like better managers of your wealth, even though they both lost money in year four. However, neither of them was able to compound their simple return over five years and, Manager C barely made any compound return at all over the five-year period!

Such are the vagaries of just looking at a few annual returns to choose a manager.

Best Investors Insight 17: To assess managers effectively, look at multiple years of compounded returns and additional metrics.

Short-term returns tell you very little or can be completely misleading.

This also shows how a *low-risk* approach can be part of what it takes to accumulate *higher* long-term wealth.

Losses are far more harmful to long-term returns than most investors understand. A loss is asymmetrically worse than the same amount of gain for your long-term wealth accumulation.

The five-year compounded return comparisons show that losses in any year, or at any time, can be devastating for an investor's long-term return. They are disproportionately damaging, as they require disproportionate gains to offset the losses. Even then, no account has been made for the time it took for both the drawdown and the full recovery of capital loss. There was a zero return for that time period. So, a further additional gain is then required to make up for no return over the whole period.

For example, let's assume that a modest 4 percent gain per

year is the benchmark for the managers above. However, what if a manager loses 20 percent in one year? How much return would he have to make in the following year to get back on track with a 4 percent compound rate over the full two-year period?

Answer: A 20 percent loss takes the value of one hundred down to eighty. To return to one hundred, the manager needs a 25 percent return (100/80 = 1.25). Then the investor would still lose two years of 4 percent compounded return to achieve the benchmark. So, to get back to the benchmark, the manager would need to make 35 percent (1.25 × 1.04 × 1.04 = 1.352) to make up for a 20 percent loss. Almost twice the loss!

That is a tall order for just a year, but if the manager can't do it, the deficit keeps rising, and the makeup gain gets bigger. The manager is now compounding on a lower amount of capital. The longer it takes to make back the compound returns required, the further behind they'll get.

Most likely, the loss will never be recovered without excessive risk-taking, which could land the investor in an even deeper hole. Even with just a 10 percent loss, a manager would have to make over 20 percent (100/90 × 1.04 × 1.04) in the following year to make up for it in the next year.

Best Investors Insight 18: Losses are devastating to

long-term compounded returns; as a rule of thumb, an annual return needs twice the annual gain to make up for the loss.

So, a lower-risk manager may, in fact, increase the likelihood of long-term wealth accumulation simply by avoiding that big loss! Not what many investors understand or believe!

Investors need to be aware that some levels of loss or drawdown of their account put them in a potentially permanent predicament with regard to achieving an acceptable long-term return, even at a modest 4 percent rate. This means that losses at a certain level effectively constitute a permanent impairment of opportunity for their potential long-term rate of return.

Best Investors Insight 19: Real-time information on your portfolio risk and losses and how your manager addressed it is an essential tool that investors need to monitor in their own best interest.

Investors need to know immediately if their account is no longer on track for long-term compounding. How did your portfolio do in Q4 2018 and Q1 2020?

Without monitoring risk, you have no clear idea, either in advance or in real time, whether or not you are on the path of a Best Investor or even possibly in line for an acceptable long-term return. You have no clear criteria for assessing whether a manager is acceptable. This is why, to safeguard your interest, the initial and ongoing risk report assessment should be your priority.

Best Investors Insight 20: Risk is what you actually experience and need to manage in your portfolio in real time.

Risk is not a number made up for an investor or guessed at for a portfolio. These are static, opinion-driven preconceptions.

No one knows what the future will bring or when these assessments become no longer appropriate.

Risk and drawdown must be disclosed so that, far beyond returns, you clearly understand how your portfolio is performing and what that means for your long-term compounding. Only then can you appropriately determine your long-term probability of success and whether you need to make significant management changes before too much damage has been done.

Best Investors Insight 21: Return variability also impacts compounding.

This is a major limitation of any model projecting flat rates of compounding over multi-decade periods, as is standard practice in financial planning.

Through any investment conditions, consistent returns compound at a faster rate than highly variable returns! Manager A outperformed the other managers but failed to beat the 4 percent compound rate over five years of 21.67 percent. That was only a small miss, compared to 21.5 percent, but the more variable the returns are, the greater the miss, and over long periods with greater variability, this can become a much wider gap.

For long-term planning, over ten or even thirty years, this can become a huge factor between reality and compounded projections at a single rate. In reality, real results may be materially lower relative to the stable rate projections if the variability is relatively high. This is another, perhaps more subtle factor in favor of lower risk.

Once again, a low-risk manager will outperform in the long term, just on the basis of lower return variability.

SUMMARY

Very little is more important when it comes to investing than understanding the dynamics of risk and return and how to use these two crucial concepts to your best advantage.

- Best Investors Insight 15: Best Investors have rejected the widely used theory that higher risk is linked to higher return (as shown in the previous chapter). Finding out more about the evidence and math of your underlying investment assumptions is strongly advised before you invest.

- Best Investors Insight 16: Behavioral economics and evidence suggest that higher volatility generally corresponds with FALLING asset prices.

- Best Investors Insight 17: To assess managers effectively, look at multiple years of compounded returns and additional metrics. Short-term returns tell you very little or can be completely misleading.

- Best Investors Insight 18: Losses are devastating to long-term compounded returns; as a rule of thumb, an annual return needs twice the annual gain to make up for the loss.

- Best Investors Insight 19: Real-time information on your portfolio risk and losses and how your manager addressed it is an essential tool that investors need to monitor in their own best interest.

- Best Investors Insight 20: Risk is what you actually experience and need to manage in your portfolio in real time.

- Best Investors Insight 21: Return variability also impacts compounding. This is a major limitation of any model projecting flat rates of compounding over multi-decade periods, as is standard practice in financial planning.

The next chapter thinks through the consequences of a new and different set of assessment metrics and shows how to report the key data in just one simple chart so that you're clear on how your investments are performing.

CHAPTER 7

EMPOWER YOURSELF THROUGH MEASUREMENT

"The way to attain truly superior long-term returns is to grind it out until you're up 30 or 40 percent, and then if you have the conviction, go for a 100 percent year. If you can put together a few near-100 percent years and avoid down years, then you can achieve really outstanding long-term returns."

—STAN DRUCKENMILLER

Stan Druckenmiller has one of the best trading records in history.[17] He suggests that his outstanding returns come from first generating some gains from the "grind" of alpha investing with relatively low risk. The capital gain from this can be used as capital for much bigger bets. He expects to make huge gains in some years with this approach, but

---

17   See Alex Barrow, "Lessons from a trading great: Stanley Druckenmiller," Macro Ops, December 7, 2016, https://macro-ops.com/lessons-from-a-trading-great-stanley-druckenmiller/.

if the big bets don't work out, he will only lose part of his "grind" investing capital, so he'll avoid a loss. Either way, Druckenmiller's account never stops compounding. The most remarkable part about his performance over thirty years is that his up years also came with *zero* down years. Using both alpha and capital preservation, he shows how to safely invest for outstanding, long-term returns.

This is very comparable with Jim Simon's returns, shown at the beginning of chapter 3. Consistently high returns, with just one tiny loss in only one year. The priority and execution of capital preservation are clear in both of these great investors. These returns demonstrate *both* low risk *and* high alpha. This would have been clear even from the early stages of their incredible multi-decade performance.

John Meriwether, however, clearly strayed into the "gamble" quadrant of risk and return. It was exciting for a while but ultimately, a spectacular failure. On examination, I would argue LTCM had even strayed into "avoid" despite those previous spectacular returns.

As an investor, it is crucial to understand which journey you are on—are you headed for Jim Simons' long-term returns or an LTCM wipeout? Just looking at three years of spectacular returns at LTCM would have badly misled you. Realizing that risk was high would have alerted a Best Investor to examine both the risk level and whether the alpha was really there. Any examination of LTCM would then have revealed that the high returns were a function of excessive leverage and risk, not a skillful allocation of risk for repeatable return. Alpha was not there. Credible and durable risk management was clearly absent.

Best Investors Insight 22: By the time your long-term returns turn out to be either a great success or a complete failure, it's far too late to do anything about it. You can only tell whether you are on the right track by measuring the skill of the process from risk and return to risk.

To truly measure the skill of the process, you need a risk and return performance grid.

Best Investors Insight 23: The "Risk and Return" performance grid provides the minimum information necessary for an investor to begin to understand the quality of the investment process in their own account.

The measurements in this grid are crucial for your long-term prosperity, and they are easy to report in a simple way so that, in a few seconds, you can immediately see the kind of journey your finances are taking. This grid assesses your account in real time, so that you can immediately get your own Best Investor ranking. This ranking is objective and judgment-free and empowers you by showing you exactly where you stand in terms of portfolio performance. The data needed to put this grid together is easily available, so you can and should demand it from your investment team.

COMPONENTS OF A "RISK AND RETURN" PERFORMANCE GRID

Let's look at what information can be reported and how this can be shown. The metrics described in this section are the same as those used by the Best Investors. You can use these metrics both to filter your investment choice in advance *and* to monitor the results in real time to ensure you stay on track. You can also be clear when and why you might need to significantly change your investment approach.

So, in order to have a good basic understanding of your investment performance, you just need two metrics that you can place on a grid with two axes:

1. The return (the vertical axis on the next chart)
2. The daily volatility of your return over the period (the horizontal axis on the chart)

Remember, it is not hard to get this data, so if any counterparty stands in your way, you need to have a clear conversation with them.

Then, on the same grid, you can place a dot representing both your return and the volatility of "your portfolio." On the chart, this is the circular dot. This is an example of a theoretical return for educational purposes:

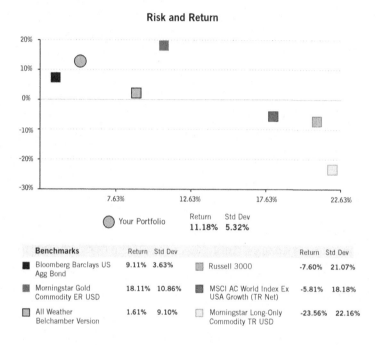

Risk and Return

	Return	Std Dev
Your Portfolio	11.18%	5.32%

Benchmarks	Return	Std Dev		Return	Std Dev
Bloomberg Barclays US Agg Bond	9.11%	3.63%	Russell 3000	-7.60%	21.07%
Morningstar Gold Commodity ER USD	18.11%	10.86%	MSCI AC World Index Ex USA Growth (TR Net)	-5.81%	18.18%
All Weather Belchamber Version	1.61%	9.10%	Morningstar Long-Only Commodity TR USD	-23.56%	22.16%

Then you can plot, on the same graph, a range of benchmark indexes with the same information on the graph. In the chart above, the different squares represent the same information, but for each benchmark for the same period, so you can see the context of your own portfolio return and risk relative to a range of benchmarks. Each benchmark is listed below the chart with their actual data.

The one exception is the "All Weather Belchamber Version," which is a composite of the other benchmarks as follows:

ASSET CLASS	% IN BENCHMARK
US bonds	45
US equities	30
World Equities EX US growth	10
Gold	10
Commodities	5

The percentages above are a long-term reference benchmark asset allocation. This does not need to confine actual allocation at any point. Allocation to any asset class may still vary from 0 percent to 100 percent.

The value of the benchmarks is to provide guidance to allow the investor an opportunity to put portfolio performance in context with general market behavior over the assessment period.

The squares in the chart show benchmark results for a range of well-known indexes representing different asset classes. The investor can immediately see what happened in the market and in their portfolio over the six-quarter assessment period (October 1, 2018 through March 31, 2020) both in terms of performance and risk.

How did the investor do?

As described in chapter 3, growth in the US peaked in Q3 2018. Not surprisingly, therefore, this was a good period for bonds and gold relative to equities and commodities. A significant alpha and low-risk Best Investor opportunity.

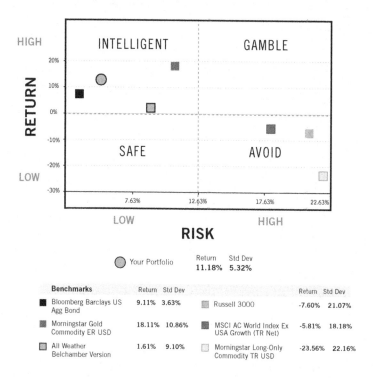

	Return	Std Dev
Your Portfolio	11.18%	5.32%

Benchmarks	Return	Std Dev		Return	Std Dev
Bloomberg Barclays US Agg Bond	9.11%	3.63%	Russell 3000	-7.60%	21.07%
Morningstar Gold Commodity ER USD	18.11%	10.86%	MSCI AC World Index Ex USA Growth (TR Net)	-5.81%	18.18%
All Weather Belchamber Version	1.61%	9.10%	Morningstar Long-Only Commodity TR USD	-23.56%	22.16%

You have the high-risk benchmarks, which are US equities (Russell 3000), Commodities (Morningstar Long-Only Commodity), and Global Equities (MSCI World Index), all of which experienced negative returns over the eighteen-month period. Gold has less volatility but still more than that of the aggregate benchmark. Gold was the clear outperformer with almost a 20 percent gain.

In the low-risk area, to the left of the aggregate benchmark, stands bonds and the portfolio.

It is possible to immediately get an assessment of how the investor did over the period based on Best Investor concepts and criteria:

1. Risk was kept below the aggregate benchmark on average over the period when risk assets did poorly.
   ◦ Check!
2. Return to risk was clearly higher than most benchmarks and comparable to the best performing benchmarks: bonds and gold. The portfolio sits on the line between bonds and gold. Compared to the benchmark index, the portfolio has both a much higher return, together with much lower risk. This represents substantial alpha.
   ◦ Check!
3. The portfolio is also well into the "Intelligent" part of the concept box.
   ◦ Check!
4. The portfolio outperformed the aggregate benchmark by more than 9 percent per annum over the period. It also outperformed all the other benchmarks except gold.
   ◦ Check!

On all the key criteria, the portfolio outperformed. The investor now knows that not only did his portfolio perform well, but he is on track for continued good performance in line with the best practices of the Best Investors. There is significant evidence of a very successful process from the manager.

Naturally, there is a whole range of metrics that can be used to look at performance. To some extent, the more, the better. These results were easy to create, as all they needed was the standard deviation of each element, in addition to the return. Drawdown can also be easily added in to the risk assessment. It is easily visible from any chart of portfolio value and is increasingly included in standard reporting.

The chart showed what happened over the period on average. There are other wider and deeper ways to look at returns by calculating some of the dynamics of what happened over the period. I am in favor of full and deep disclosure, but further analysis can be more complicated to produce, and that typically comes with greater expense.

LIMITATIONS OF BENCHMARKS

Benchmarks are just a first guide—they only go so far. They should be used as a form of measurement and guidance, not as an objective and direct comparison to one's portfolio. To truly understand this, it's necessary to recognize the limitations of benchmarks.

While benchmarks provide a quick first take, they don't go far in providing a full assessment. Take an extreme example. No one is likely to thank an investment advisor for a great job in losing only 40 percent of their capital because a benchmark was down 50 percent. So, any direct return comparison between benchmarks and portfolio returns fails to take into account of a manager's ability to manage risk or have some portfolio diversification, among other factors over the long term.

For this reason, in a bull market, portfolios may not keep up with the 100 percent invested position in a single benchmark. Equally, a portfolio should outperform on the downside. The key is how the portfolio performs over a full cycle or through all the cycles on Best Investor criteria. What is quickly revealed is the extent to which your account is aligned with Best Investor criteria, which is far more important than return and which you can also see.

By the same token, if your portfolio simply replicates some combination of the key benchmarks, then you can also see to what extent the manager is doing anything different from some static allocation to some benchmarks. In this case, the manager is offering very little beyond what the investor could do themself.

Returns below benchmarks are the usual result. Costs and fees clearly play a key role, particularly for mutual funds, and so there should be some recognition of the cost differential between the benchmarks and the portfolio.

What is rare is high return to risk portfolio returns, which, in addition, are above benchmarks.

In order to generate high return to risk outcomes above benchmarks, capital has to be managed highly efficiently and effectively. No passive allocation to low-cost benchmarks could have replicated high return to risk without being in the right place at the right time and/or not in the wrong place at the wrong time. Furthermore, an excess return over benchmarks has, in addition, exceeded any costs. As shown previously, this is an additional hurdle, which reflects either, or both, low costs or effective risk management.

This should empower you to have a much better idea of how your portfolio is really doing. Then you can have a far more productive conversation with your manager and a much better idea of the extent to which your best interests are being met. You are no longer dependent on the description your advisor provides because you have the data, and you know how to use it! As a result, the investor is in charge, and the conversation is much more productive.

Investors no longer need to discuss "the market" or allocation to the same extent. Investors now see key components of the process and can raise the discussion to the level of Best Investors. The process and contribution of the manager become more clearly defined. The investor will make better decisions with better information.

SUMMARY

- Best Investors Insight 22: By the time your long-term returns turn out to be a great success or a complete failure, it's far too late to do anything about it. You can only tell whether you are on the right track or in time to alter course by measuring the skill of the process from risk and return to risk.

- Best Investors Insight 23: The risk and return performance grid provides the minimum information necessary for an investor to begin to understand the quality of the investment process in their own account.

It's easy to construct the risk and return performance grid, and it then quickly reveals the criteria used by the Best Investors.

Now, the investor is armed with new tools and insights. It is possible to use these tools to examine different strategies and see the strengths and weaknesses more clearly. Then investors are better able to choose the best strategies for themselves.

The next chapter critically analyzes two investment strategies based on Best Investor criteria. Do established approaches stand up to Best Investor scrutiny? Should low-risk approaches be dismissed as they could never produce a high long-term return?

CHAPTER 8

KNOW THE INVESTMENT MYTHS AND HERESIES WITH BEST INVESTOR ANALYSIS

"Along with this idea as to what constituted the basis for common-stock selection emerged a companion theory that common stocks represented the most profitable and therefore the most desirable media for long-term investment. This gospel was based on a certain amount of research, showing that diversified lists of common stocks had regularly increased in value over stated intervals of time for many years past.

"These statements sound innocent and plausible. Yet they concealed two theoretical weaknesses that could and did result in untold mischief. The first of these defects was that they abolished the fundamental distinctions between investment and speculation. The second was that they ignored the

price of a stock in determining whether or not it was a desirable purchase.

"The notion that the desirability of a common stock was entirely independent of its price seems incredibly absurd. Yet the new-era theory led directly to this thesis... An alluring corollary of this principle was that making money in the stock market was now the easiest thing in the world. It was only necessary to buy 'good' stocks, regardless of price, and then to let nature take her upward course. The results of such a doctrine could not fail to be tragic."

—BENJAMIN GRAHAM AND DAVID L. DODD, *SECURITY ANALYSIS*, 1934

The chapters in Part II have now provided powerful information and criteria to examine the math, facts, and evidence on which different strategies are based. In this chapter, then, we're ready to critically examine two investment approaches to reveal how Best Investor analysis can transform your investment perspective.

The first strategy we'll examine is the buy-and-hold investment strategy. Financial advisors commonly recommend buy-and-hold portfolios or some variation of passive investing as a basic strategy. This approach takes the view that long-term investment is the primary focus, and so all buys should be held for the long term and only reviewed at portfolio review meetings. This involves very little time and attention, and it would be great if it worked well. It is worth analyzing how passive buy-and-hold investing measures up. What are the pros and cons? Is it a false myth that decisions should be solely made at portfolio meetings?

Benjamin Graham's comments show that this behavior or strategy was also prevalent in the 1920s and why, in his opinion, "the results of such a doctrine could not fail to be tragic."

For the second investment strategy, we'll introduce a relatively new concept that is antithetical to the financial advisor's allocation bias in favor of risk. This method starts by taking a completely different route, diametrically opposite to the theory espoused by financial advisors—it purposely allocates to the *lowest* risk equities. Is that heresy? Let's take a look.

BUY AND HOLD OR PASSIVE INVESTING

The chart[18] below shows the total real return (dividends included) of $1,000 invested in the S&P 500. Here we are focusing solely on the equity part of the portfolio. For most investors, this is a significant proportion of their allocation.

---

18 The chart is available at: Lance Roberts, "The myth of stocks for the long run—Part I," Real Investment Advice, June 4, 2018, https://realinvestmentadvice.com/the-myths-of-stocks-for-the-long-run-part-i/.

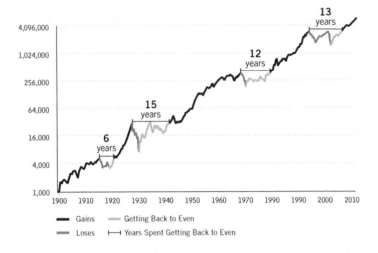

Total Real Return of $1000 Investment with DCA

What history shows is that just owning the index is a great strategy in the bull phases of the market, but it can be a dreadful one between these periods.

Between 2000 and 2013, an investor would have experienced two 50 percent drawdowns, as well as a zero return overall for thirteen years. Although the bull market years make great returns, how long beyond that thirteen-year period would an investor have to stay invested to make up for it? In many countries, the drawdown period for major stock market indexes has been more than twice as long as that. The Nikkei 225 Index in Japan is a case in point. The highs of 1989 have still not been breached over 30 years later. Who would commit themselves to a long-term allocation strategy that could end up providing no return for more than thirty years?

No manager with any risk or drawdown criteria would have survived for long, even in the first year in 2000 of this flat performance. At least this would have immediately alerted an investor to consider changing strategy. The Simple Trend System model (shown in chapter 3) did a far better job over that thirteen-year period, and any number of filters could have alerted an investor to either take action or use a completely different strategy.

Passive investing is typically popular after periods of extended good performance, but typically it has been a poor long-term allocation approach. Once again, in 2020, passive investing is very popular after a period of good long-term returns. This should therefore be a time for careful analysis, given the very poor historical precedent. Here are two charts that are worth consulting for anyone with a long-term passive investment commitment.

The first chart[19] shows the cumulative change in Real S&P 500 and real profits. Prices and profits should eventually be closely correlated. To the extent that they diverge significantly should therefore be a major factor in investment consideration.

For long-term investing, a good time to be a patient holder

---

19   This chart has been taken from an article by Lance Roberts, "Fed stimulus has created the cobra effect. 7-24-20," Real Investment Advice, July 25, 2020, https://realinvestmentadvice.com/fed-stimulus-has-created-the-cobra-effect-07-24-20.

of equities would be following a period when the S&P 500 Index has been underperforming real profits, as in the early 1980s. Equally, it has been a poor time for long-term investing when the S&P 500 Index can be observed as having already outperformed real profits, as in the late 1960s, 2000, and 2007. Notice that this is also a period of significant outperformance of the S&P 500 Index.

Cumulative Change In Real S&P 500 & Real Profits

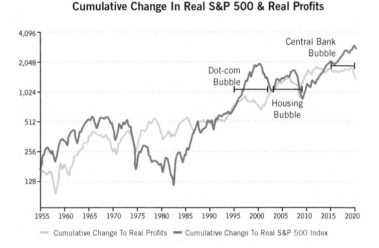

— Cumulative Change To Real Profits — Cumulative Change To Real S&P 500 Index

The second chart[20] shows the expected twelve-year return calculation, which has a great record of calculating future actual returns going back to the 1920s. This is applied to a standard portfolio allocation of 60/30/10 portfolio of the S&P 500/Treasury bonds/Treasury bills.

---

20 This chart has been taken from a blog by John P. Hussman, "Fundamentally Unsound," Hussman Funds, July 2020, https://www.hussmanfunds.com/comment/mc200712/.

Currently, this calculation suggests that expected returns for this allocation are near the worst in history and is currently projecting a negative return.

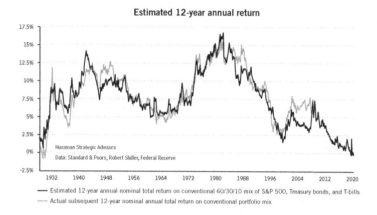

Estimated 12-year annual return

— Estimated 12-year annual nominal total return on conventional 60/30/10 mix of S&P 500, Treasury bonds, and T-bills
— Actual subsequent 12-year nominal annual total return on conventional portfolio mix

The record current allocation to passive investment strategies suggests that many investors need to carefully review the extent to which passive allocations to stocks and bonds are currently appropriate to avoid being on the high risk "gamble" or "avoid" long-term expected return outlooks without a proactive risk management strategy.

Passive investment has a range of challenges:

1. There is no proactive risk management strategy, and so investors are exposed to unacceptable losses. This violates the first principle of Best Investor criteria and puts long-term compounding at significant risk.
2. Timing the market is rejected. This assumes away a

huge amount of real-time information and price development as ever requiring a real-time asset allocation response. In what way could that be optimal? The Best Investors have multi-decade records of real-time investment activity.

3. Currently, the two charts above suggest 2020 is a challenging time to commit to passive investing. Passive investing is, in theory, a long-term strategy, yet it apparently disregards important measures of long-term expected return and value. The quote at the beginning of this chapter made a similar point over eighty years ago.

PARADOX INVESTING: HERESY THAT WORKS

The theory that high risk correlates with high return has become so ingrained in investors' thinking that to suggest a low-risk approach to investing could be better has to be introduced as some kind of paradox.

The investing website, Paradox Investing, focuses on a low-risk emphasis as the way to high returns.[21] The following chart and the great work of Pim van Vliet and Jan de Koning of Robeco in Rotterdam, Holland, are clearly outlined on the Paradox website and on the Robeco website.[22] Just the introduction to their book, *High Returns from Low Risk*,

---

21 See https://www.paradoxinvesting.com/.

22 See www.robeco.com.

refers to "evidence-based investing—applying thoroughly tested investment theories to portfolio construction." This sounds promising.

By using three factors, they find out what works best over eighty years. The three factors most highly ranked in a simple selection system with rebalancing are:

1. Low volatility
2. Income
3. Momentum

Just by rebalancing to a simple ranking system, they get what they call the "conservative stocks" portfolio.

Then they flip the priority on all three factors to create the "risky stocks" portfolio.

The illustration below shows how that turned out, and the data is downloadable on an excel spreadsheet on the website link above. So, you can check that data too!

Conservative vs. Risky

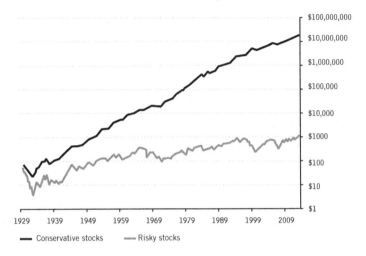

Conservative stocks ——— Risky stocks

The results show a massive difference. Investors are offered a clear indication of the durable long-term outperformance of low volatility stocks from a simple strategy clearly set out and with straightforward execution.

The news is that over eighty years, the low-risk equity factor massively outperformed the high-risk equity factor. The other factors no doubt have an influence; however, the best eighty-year results came from a low volatility priority in equity selection. Clearly, some low-volatility biased portfolios can do far better than some high-volatility portfolios.

Robeco has done a significant amount of research on how to take advantage of low volatility as a selection factor in equity portfolios. Over an eleven-year period, their conservative portfolio below shows much greater efficiency, by way of high long-term returns, with lower volatility and drawdown than alternatives. The return/risk grid[23] shows this.

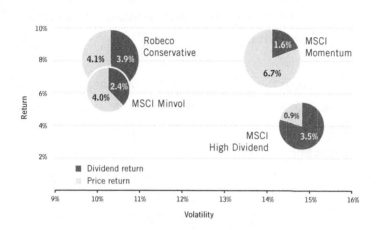

Robeco versus MSCI Factor indices, 2006-2017

Here is significant evidence that high risk is not necessarily the optimal approach that should be adopted as a factor in allocation.

The Robeco conservative strategy has a much better profile for dynamic compounding. Both higher income and lower volatility mean that dynamic compounding is far less harmed by the 2008 experience, and the further detail in

---

23   This chart is available at Pim van Vliet, "High Dividend Investing: Buy them Stable and Strong," Robeco, April 24, 2018, https://www.robeco.com/en/insights/2018/04/high-dividend-investing-buy-them-stable-and-strong.html.

the link shows that over the eleven-year period, this fund had the highest alpha and outperformed the World MSCI Index by over 2 percent per annum.

Best Investors Insight 24: Not only does passive investing involve many unresolved issues, but allocating to high risk within a passive allocation is also a highly questionable strategy.

Detailed Best Investor analysis is already suggesting that there could be more promising investment strategies than conventional thinking offers. This is just a start, and the focus of Part III.

This should not be a surprise given the work we have covered in Part II and the insights from the Best Investors. Compounding is where the great returns come from. Low risk is essential to compounding.

"Without capital Preservation, there is no compounding."

—DIEGO PARRILLA

SUMMARY

- Best Investors Insight 24: Not only does passive investing involve many unresolved issues, but allocating to high risk within a passive allocation is also a highly questionable strategy.

Passive investing does not measure up to Best Investor criteria, and equity drawdown periods have lasted much longer than a decade in the US and for over thirty years in Japan.

Eighty-year US equity data analysis again challenges the assumption that higher-risk strategies generate higher longer-term returns.

A new heretical focus on low-risk strategies shows evidence that low risk is paradoxically a better way to achieve higher long-term returns.

Evidence for new investment thinking comes from:

1. The Best Investors
2. The dynamics of compound interest
3. New evidence from eighty years of data suggest that low volatility equities are the best volatility selection focus for higher long-term returns

Once you bring this degree of clarity from the math and evidence of risk and return, you'll find a remarkable resonance exists between lower risk and higher alpha. The natural consequence of this powerful insight then flows through high probability compounding to high long-term returns.

In Part III, you'll learn how to *Invest Like the Best*.

PART III

INVEST LIKE
THE BEST

In the first line of the introduction to this book, I set the objective and made the claim that: "I will guide you through the wisdom needed to generate and preserve wealth."

By the end of Part II, this had already been established, and Part III will build on this insight. What I did not explain is that preservation and growth go together. They are inter-twined. This idea is not an opinion; it is simply embedded in the mathematical dynamics of compound interest. It's not hidden from anyone; it's just not seen, understood, and optimally practiced by almost everyone.

The Best Investors understand this and know how to develop this natural insight better than anyone else.

This is a major transformation in standard investment thinking. So often, investors are asked to choose between either preservation *or* growth. They are normally regarded as separate options. Best Investor metrics are crystal clear that preservation is always a factor in every decision, and it resonates with high alpha and high long-term returns.

It's time to focus on actual investment decisions.

In Part I and Part II, we've established the foundations you need for best investing, starting with your mindset and moving on to principles, objectives, and measurements for best investing approaches.

Now it's time to put those foundations to use. Part III explores the techniques and insights that help get to the most optimal practices.

Decisions, strategies, and execution flow easily from what was established in the first two parts. Rather than limit how we can execute, the crystal clear definition about principles, priorities, metrics, and measurements not only keeps you on track for a transformative outcome, they provide a productive focus simply by following Best Investor practices.

What happens very naturally, it seems, is that lower risk seems to go with higher alpha and long-term returns almost wherever we look. This is a step-by-step process, and there are still some final pieces and additional tools that can be added over the last leg of the journey.

CHAPTER 9

MONEY MANAGEMENT MATTERS

"Investors spend a ton of time vetting ideas and building their thesis around that idea. But when it comes time to actually put on a trade, most investors don't have a framework for sizing that position, which is equally critical to the success of that investment."

—KEITH MCCULLOUGH

There are two very different elements to investing or trading a portfolio:

1. Asset and security selection
2. Money management—how much you buy or sell and when you execute a trade

Of the two, money management may be more important.

In fact, you can do very well without even any of your own asset or security selection.

In this chapter, the only security selection we'll use is the publicly available positions taken by billionaires. It demonstrates how much performance improvement the billionaires could have made just by using Best Investor based money management rules.

Now that we are going to "invest like the best," let's be clear. Every tool or technique adopted is designed to either lower risk or increase alpha. Both would be even better. There are many approaches to this, and investors should choose what serves them best. For the purpose of this example, I will adopt the TradeStops system.

MORE ABOUT TREND, VOLATILITY, AND TRAILING STOPS

TradeStops, founded by Dr. Richard Smith, is a Software as a Service (SaaS) program that helps individual investors mitigate risk and monitor their investments. TradeStops offers a series of money management tools that can transform portfolio performance. Everything is designed on Best Investor principles and objectives of containing risk while increasing alpha, and, of course, the returns flow from there.

It is quite remarkable how far this journey goes from just a simple beginning. It all starts from being able to calculate for any asset or security two key measures:

1. An optimal trend line, showing current price direction
2. An optimal volatility quotient (VQ), showing the current level of volatility

From these two measures, you automatically have a trend line that the asset is either above or below, and you have a volatility or risk measure VQ. From just these two factors, it is possible to form a complete rules-based trading system.

1. Buy when the asset closes VQ above the trend line.
2. Sell when the asset closes below the trend line (hence the name "TradeStops").

This places any security into a certain state. There is a clear buy and sell signal, and there is clarity on whether the asset should either be held or avoided. So, it introduces a Security State Indicator (SSI). Then investors can hold the investment in the buy state or go to cash when it goes below the trend line and is therefore in the sell state. In other words, the whole process of investing can become systematized, which fits in with our investment mindset framework outlined in chapter 2.

Immediately, it is possible to see the benefit. Backtesting is never perfectly definitive; however, when used appropriately, it does provide significant evidence about whether a system may or may not have merit. The next chart shows that, instead of just staying invested in the S&P 500 for eighteen years from 1999 through 2017, this simple SSI system would have minimized losses and drawdown instead by reducing risk *and* increasing return. Immediately, we are shown that this simple system reduces risk and increases return to risk to such an extent that the long-term return is far higher.

The chart compares the S&P 500 Index with "SPY with SSI" (SPY is the tradeable form of the S&P 500 Index, with the SSI system applied to it).[24] As you can see, it goes to cash when the sell signal is triggered until the buy signal is triggered the next time. This produces significant outperformance with lower risk metrics.

Net Gains

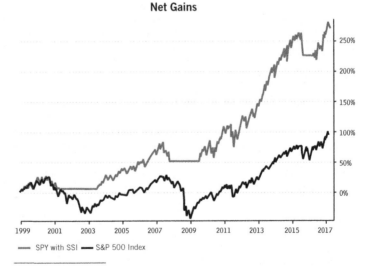

— SPY with SSI — S&P 500 Index

---

24   The chart is available at TradeSmith Education, "The TradeStops Strategies, Part I," *TradeStops by TradeSmith*, July 17, 2017, https://tradestops.com/blog/tradestops-strategies-part-1/.

Of course, there are many different configurations that can be backtested for profit efficiency, but immediately it is possible to see how the standard metrics for TradeStops can improve long-term return. Naturally, to be statistically significant, it needs to be tested in a much larger sample base of securities.

If you're looking for more detailed analysis, TradeStops blog "Strategies Part II"[25] is a good source.

PORTFOLIO MONEY MANAGEMENT

These simple concepts can then be applied to portfolios as well. The history of billionaires' positions is publicly disclosed and therefore readily available for examination and testing. The following chart summarizes the results of what could have been achieved simply from a basic money management rules-based system.

As the chart also shows, the billionaires did much better than the S&P 500 over the eighteen-year period, almost doubling the long-term return. That being said, simply by using the "Quant Tool" on all the billionaire portfolios more than triples the long-term return.

The quant tool simply buys and sells the same positions on

---

25   TradeSmith Education, "The TradeStops Strategies, Part 2," *TradeStops by TradeSmith*, July 24, 2017, https://tradestops.com/blog/tradestops-strategies-part-2/.

the same day as the billionaires. The main difference is that
position sizing is applied, weighting positions in favor of
low-risk securities and adding in trailing stops, plus a few
other low-risk additional measures.

So, once again, every step reduces risk, with the great benefit of increasing the long-term return.

Finally, the "4 Billionaire PQ (Pure Quant)" portfolio even
manages to almost triple the quant tool approach. This is
achieved by optimizing the selection of which billionaire
portfolios are included in the mix.[26]

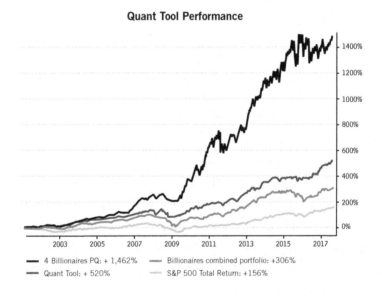

Quant Tool Performance

— 4 Billionaires PQ: + 1,462%   — Billionaires combined portfolio: +306%
— Quant Tool: + 520%   — S&P 500 Total Return: +156%

---

26 This chart is available at TradeStops Research Team, "Four billionaires, four investment styles,
one incredible result," *TradeStops by TradeSmith*, April 10, 2018, https://tradestops.com/blog/
four-billionaires-four-investment-styles-one-incredible-result/.

These results show the significant efficiency of using a money management system for your portfolio investments. This is a full rules-based system, and it is instructive to review its filters. The main systematic approaches adopted were:

1. Optimized trend
2. Volatility Quotient (VQ) defining buy and sell signals
3. Position sizing by VQ in favor of *low-volatility* assets in the portfolio
4. Entirely eliminating very high-volatility stocks

It has already become a common theme that lowering risk in a variety of ways can also lead to higher long-term returns.

Some further measures were also used to minimize risk and improve return:

1. Only buy stocks newly in an uptrend
2. Eliminate laggards that are not higher from their entry point when rebalancing is done—a momentum requirement

Some possible adjustments include:

1. Varying the number of stocks in the portfolio
2. Examining the "Low Covariance" selection discussed

in chapter 10, which introduces a bias in favor of uncorrelated stocks—even occasionally with higher volatility—from different sectors without increasing portfolio volatility and potentially increasing return

The usual qualifications should be added in here too. To the extent that optimization could be used, there is always the risk of some "curve fitting," or in other words, fitting the model to the specific data rather than applying it to random data. This means there is some risk that the data looks better than it is because the data is then not random relative to the factors optimized in the model. To the extent this is the case, the results will look better than reality. However, only steps seven and eight were optimized on the billionaire's data. Overall, the numbers still indicate what a rules-based money management system can do to improve returns.[27]

The example shows the kind of multiple steps that can be employed to improve portfolio returns just with money management rules. It also shows the value of emphasizing low-risk strategies, not just in trailing stops, but also in a range of portfolio criteria to improve long-term returns.

---

27   For more information on the Quant Tool, see TradeSmith Education, "Pure Quant—Rules-based investing from TradeStops," *TradeStops by TradeSmith*, June 5, 2017, https://tradestops.com/blog/pure-quant-rules-based-investing-tradestops/.

SUMMARY

Money management rules applied to a number of different assets and equities showed a significant transformation in results just by adopting Best Investor practices. Why would anyone *not* want to get both lower risk and higher long-term returns just from a systemic approach to money management?

Consider the benefits you can achieve solely from money management rules. It is too significant an investment factor not to be conscious of the role it can play in your portfolio management and not to have a clear sense of the system and its effects on your portfolio.

Minimum volatility techniques also continue to show significant benefit.

In the next chapter, we'll discuss these questions: Are there simple tools or tradeable portfolios like **Exchange-Traded Funds (ETF)** that can be used to take advantage of low risk and high alpha? Covariance is a key component in minimum volatility portfolios; how does that add to portfolio construction? What is the best portfolio construction for long-term returns?

CHAPTER 10

INVESTMENT ALLOCATION

"A portfolio manager must understand that safeguarding against loss does not end with finding the perfect security at the perfect price. If it did, then the perfect portfolio would likely consist of one security. Rather, to the extent possible, I have the responsibility to structure the portfolio such that if any of a number of unforeseen events occur, that I do not lose the whole, or even a significant portion, of the client's money. To do this, I seek to minimize the correlation between the intrinsic values of the various securities held in the portfolio."

—MICHAEL BURRY

"If you don't own [gold]...there is no sensible reason other than you don't know history or you don't know the economics of it..."

—RAY DALIO

As you've seen, a focus on minimum volatility strategies is a highly effective factor in ensuring higher long-term returns, but also with lower risk. What could be a better way to compound your returns?

The next chart[28] illustrates the impact of using low covariance (low internal correlation between assets in a portfolio) and how it changes the concept of risk and long-term return in a remarkably favorable way. It is possible to shift outcomes towards *both* higher return *and* lower risk.

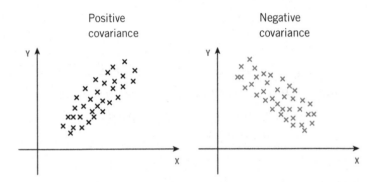

On the positive covariance side of the chart, higher returns (on the y-axis) are correlated with higher volatility or positive covariance (on the x-axis). This was, or still is, a common assumption. What these minimum volatility techniques show is that this relationship can be altered in a much more beneficial way. The negative covariance side shows that, with Best Investor criteria, investors can have both lower risk and/or higher return.

---

28 This chart is available at: "Preprocessing for deep learning: from covariance matrix to image whitening," Data Science Central, August 28, 2018, https://www.datasciencecentral.com/profiles/blogs/preprocessing-for-deep-learning-from-covariance-matrix-to-image.

Best Investors believe in the right side of the chart. Many financial advisors and investors believe in the left side of the chart.

Asset management is increasingly seeing the value of minimum volatility strategies. Funds are now being dedicated to using low volatility as the main factor in generating higher long-term returns. For example, iShares, one of the world's largest providers of Exchange-Traded Funds (ETF), has produced a series of minimum volatility ETFs to spread this approach more widely, so investors now have one-click access to funds biased on a low volatility concept.

iShares' minimum volatility ETFs show that, even over the eight-year equity bull market from 2011, all four main ETFs designed this way had either similar or better returns across the globe and, in every case, much lower volatility.

As you can see from the next chart,[29] even in a bull market for equities, the arrows move from the lower right to the upper left, just like the negative covariance chart above. Once again, the benefit is clear and shows how Best Investor criteria can work in practice. These minimum volatility charts only use some of the measures described in the previous chapter, so the angle of the low covariance

---

29   This chart and the minimum volatility table are available at "A new portfolio approach: Minimum volatility ETFs for the core of your portfolio," iShares by Blackrock, https://www.ishares.com/us/literature/investor-guide/ishares-minimum-volatility-investor-guide-us-en.pdf.

improvement could be steeper and higher to the left with additional measures.

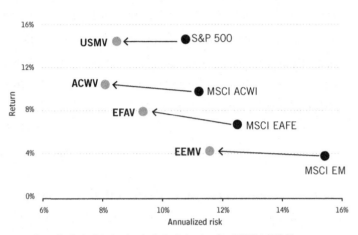

iShares Edge Minimum Volatility ETFs:
A Track Record of Market-Like Returns with Less Risk

Source: Morningstar. Data shown based on fund and index returns from 11/01/11 to 12/31/19.

Adopting minimum volatility strategies as replacements for standard index-based ETFs has significant benefits. The next chart shows that for a standard portfolio allocation, the same version replaced with minimum volatility ETFs outperforms on all metrics shown.

The graphic below illustrates the potential impact of replacing a traditional equity portfolio with minimum volatility ETFs. Over the period analyzed, risk-adjusted returns improved and drawdowns were reduced by more than 50%, demonstrating the potential benefits of using minimum volatility ETFs as a core equity replacement.

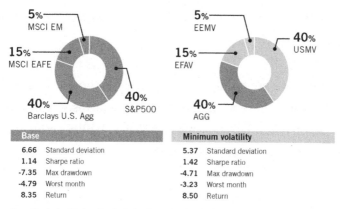

Base		Minimum volatility	
6.66	Standard deviation	5.37	Standard deviation
1.14	Sharpe ratio	1.42	Sharpe ratio
-7.35	Max drawdown	-4.71	Max drawdown
-4.79	Worst month	-3.23	Worst month
8.35	Return	8.50	Return

Source: Morningstar. Data shown based on fund and index returns from 11/01/11 - 12/31/19.

What has become clear is the double compounding benefit of using Best Investor criteria.

Lower drawdowns and higher alpha are going to compound at a faster rate. In addition, this kind of investment management is much easier to live with, as it involves much less stress and greater stability. This makes for better financial planning and means greater financial security.

Continuing our journey deeper into this subject, it is worth pointing out that part of the mathematical power of portfolio construction used by these minimum volatility ETFs is low covariance, a key component of portfolio efficiency and system design.

COVARIANCE

MSCI Minimum Volatility Indexes are designed to provide the lowest return variance for a given covariance matrix of stock returns.[30]

While there are a number of factors that go into the construction of these minimum volatility indexes, covariance is a main feature in lowering portfolio volatility far beyond just choosing low volatility stocks.

Low covariance means achieving lower portfolio volatility by choosing portfolio constituents that do not move in the same direction at the same time. In fact, the less they move together, the better, and it can be ideal if they move in opposite directions at the same time.

Stocks and bonds are often mixed in a portfolio because they often have low covariance. When that is the case, a portfolio of stocks and bonds will have lower volatility than a portfolio of just stocks. However, this feature goes far beyond just stocks and bonds.

This is a key factor not only in portfolio construction but also system design. One reason why the Simple Trend System shown in chapter 3 worked so well was that the system only used three asset classes, all of which typically

---

30 For more on covariance, see "MSCI USA Minimum Volatility Index (USD)," MSCI, September 30, 2020, https://www.msci.com/documents/10199/f5c0900d-ab44-4bdd-bec7-94761d009094.

have low correlation. The other reason is that the trend system used momentum and sell stops. Clearly, a sell stop has lower volatility and drawdown than buy and hold.

As we reach deeper into portfolio design, we begin to see multiple factors in play. It soon becomes not just one technique, but how combinations of rules and factors make portfolios and systems work so well. A Best Investor is constantly searching for the best combination of these factors, and low covariance is a powerful tool in that search.

COVARIANCE AS THE "HOLY GRAIL"

Many investors consider low covariance as the "holy grail" of portfolio investing. Ray Dalio, the founder and CIO of one of the world's largest hedge funds over a multi-decade period, explains why in an excellent Investopedia video.[31]

We'll now dive into some of the models and methods developed with low covariance at their core.

RAY DALIO'S "ALL WEATHER" ALLOCATION

Ray Dalio's great insight in the 1970s was that gold had low covariance compared to other asset classes. Through this insight, he was able to construct what became known as

---

31 Investopedia, "Ray Dalio breaks down his 'Holy Grail'," YouTube, April 27, 2019, https://www. youtube.com/watch?v=Nu4lHaSh7D4&feature=youtu.be.

the "All Weather" allocation, with stocks, bonds, gold, and other low covariance assets. Dalio called it "All Weather" because the allocation model managed to produce low volatility returns that survived well through all economic conditions. His "All Weather" model became a cornerstone in developing the fund of the same name. It has grown to be one of the biggest funds within the hedge fund community.

He found that he was able to lower drawdown and volatility, and as a result, produce more stable returns with higher alpha. There are many variations of this concept, and compared to most static allocations, this usually results in a low risk and/or high alpha result. This is why I used a variation as a static allocation benchmark in chapter 7. It is typically a higher standard to beat, as well as a more stable one.

It is surprising that despite this finding in the 1970s and the continuing evidence ever since, gold still plays such a small role in most investors' portfolios. This is yet another flaw in most investors' portfolios. This is an objective statement based on math and evidence.

THE "DRAGON" PORTFOLIO

The most advanced work on low covariance assets comes from Chris Cole of Artemis Capital Management. His examination of data across eighty years of history led to the "Dragon" portfolio, which further emphasizes the use of noncorrelated assets not typically included in asset allocation models today. His analysis also agrees that gold is an important allocation. One clear concern that comes out of his work about current allocation standards in passive investment models:[32]

> "A remarkable 91% of the price appreciation for a Classic Equity and Bond Portfolio (60/40) over the past 90 years comes from just 22 years between 1984 and 2007."

This could be a case of anchoring to the recent past rather than understanding long-term secular cycles.

Balanced Risk ("Dragon") Portfolio

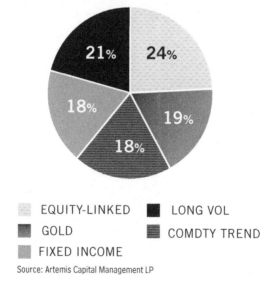

EQUITY-LINKED   LONG VOL
GOLD   COMDTY TREND
FIXED INCOME

Source: Artemis Capital Management LP

---

32   The full interview with Chris Cole is at Real Vision Finance, "How to build a recession-proof investment portfolio (w/Danielle DiMartino-Booth and Chris Cole)" YouTube, March 12, 2020, https://www.youtube.com/watch?v=SkfgEZtJ9LA.

SUMMARY

Low volatility investing has already arrived, and low covariance is another valuable tool. If you are not using low covariance in your portfolio construction, it may not be optimal. It is a natural fit for Best Investors.

The most advanced portfolio thinking includes a significant gold allocation.

The next stage of development is to take this into **Active Investment Management**. This can take investing to the next level because assets are complex and dynamic. So, the optimal portfolio addresses complexity more appropriately and must also be dynamic.

CHAPTER 11

ACTIVE INVESTMENT MANAGEMENT

"Calculus is the language of the universe as well as the logical engine for extracting its secrets."

—STEVEN STROGATZ, *INFINITE POWERS*

"To be a great long-term investor, you need to manage risk over the short-term."

—KEITH MCCULLOUGH

Active Management attempts to make consistent, short-term positive returns no matter the current economic and market conditions. In this way, performance can be managed to fit Best Investor criteria. Only then can capital preservation and compounding be delivered for optimal high long-term returns.

If active management is not adopted, it is important to consider what the alternative experience is likely to be. Looking at the long-term experience of even the most optimal static allocation portfolios, it is likely that a drawdown of at least 20 percent in a year is probable at some stage. It could be far greater if the allocation has any outsized asset concentration. Even in this best-case example, this is a problem in store for compounding for several years, as was discussed in chapters 6 and 8.

The most troubling element of the static or passive allocation approach is that there is no clear priority and so no full accountability to risk management. Risk management requires real-time, active management. Risk and opportunity are not static; they happen all the time, at any time, and with any degree of magnitude.

Any manager that commits to a static or passive investment approach is making a significant statement that downgrades the key importance of capital preservation and optimal compounding of the account value. This would not be acceptable to a Best Investor.

ACTIVE MANAGEMENT

There are, of course, many ways to go about active investment management. At the outset, it seems challenging to harness the full value of all the relevant information into a simple execution system that works effectively. However, by embracing complexity and using the most up-to-date software, all the key factors can play a part and produce a simple and executable approach, all from an evidence- and math-based process.

Calculus is just the analysis of rate of change.

The study of markets and data really is the study of analyzing data series. To be fully grounded in your conclusions, this is about the rate of continuous change and what evidence can be found to discover causation and correlation. Done effectively, this can significantly shift efficiency and probability in your favor.

There is a highly measurable interaction between economic data and market behavior. This was already revealed in chapter 3. By analyzing the data, it is clear that optimal asset allocation performance changes with economic conditions, and this can be backtested so portfolios can be aligned with economic conditions as they change. This is not a matter of academic economic theory. It is simply a matter of finding data, applying math, and examining the evidence.

CYCLES

"Rule No. 1: Most things will prove to be cyclical. Rule No. 2: Some of the greatest opportunities for gain and loss come when other people forget Rule No. 1."

—HOWARD MARKS

The "All Weather" approach, together with extensive data mining, reveal that the two key economic variables that most influence asset prices are:

1. The rate of change of inflation
2. The rate of change of economic growth

As shown in the next graphic, the rate of change of both inflation and economic growth are either both rising or both falling or moving in opposite directions in two different ways. So, the investment allocation environment can be described as having a total of four main investment conditions or quadrants:

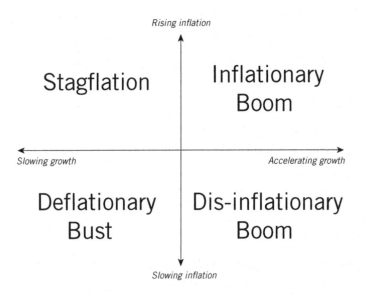

For example, equities perform better when growth is rising, and government bonds do well when both growth and inflation is falling. The data can be analyzed going back for decades to test for the best allocation across all asset classes for each of the four quadrants.

Over time, growth and inflation will constantly shift, and as they do, the optimal allocation will also shift. The cycles of growth and inflation can be measured and mapped by data, enabling us to analyze and interpret patterns of historical data. It is then possible to see how cycles evolve, detect their trends, and keep track of their changes. This can all be combined into an active investment system.

For an up-to-date example of how this can work in practice, look to Hedgeye, which provides great transparency regarding their work in this area. In the video "How I built my wealth without huge drawdowns,"[33] Hedgeye Risk Management Founder Keith McCullough talks you through his active management system in practice. I highly recommend watching the full video for his insight and clarity, but I'll provide a few slides to provide an introduction.

Economic cycles turn slowly and predictably, so time series can be created to provide high probability economic estimates for direction and the rate of change of key variables. This was introduced in chapter 3. It showed that the

---

33 Hedgeye, "Webcast [Replay] McCullough: How I built my wealth without huge drawdowns," YouTube, November 6, 2018, https://www.youtube.com/watch?v=hS-JOXZrcdU&list=PLuhl1D-19WCm4Afg7yfw7b6B4Ej24WdNA&index=32&t=296s.

direction of cycles can be estimated with high probability months in advance.

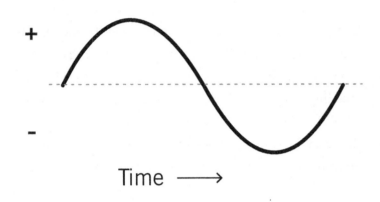

This approach is fact- and math-based, so it is free of human decision flaws or economic theory. The approach provides systematic signals to enable an investor to reposition a portfolio for significant shifts in the economic cycle well in advance of the market response.

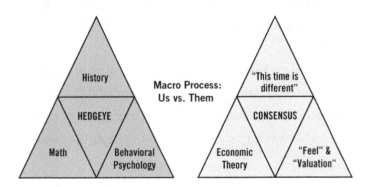

In many ways, the Hedgeye approach embodies the discoveries discussed in chapter 2 and shows the great contrast with a more conventional framework. They have taken these insights to a very high level of development.

Chapter 3 showed how declining growth and inflation was indicated for Q4 2018 more than three months in advance. This gave plenty of time to transition the portfolio to a different allocation.

This principle can be applied across all asset classes for changing allocations at any time as the economy moves across the four-quadrant economic cycle. Backtesting provides a valuable guide to what works best in different quadrants. This analysis can be taken down to micro levels of analysis, subsectors of the markets, and even into individual equity allocation.

This economic model provides a framework for asset allocation that can be updated in real time and can be used in combination with trading models.

TRADING MODELS

Expanding computing power and declining commissions in recent decades have led to significant growth and innovation in trading software development. Investors have new opportunities to invest that were never available before.

Whatever trading models are used, they can be tailored to fit Best Investor criteria. It is well worth finding the most effective trading systems as the markets have become increasingly complicated, interconnected, and sensitive across asset classes and geographically.

HOW TO COMBINE ECONOMICS WITH MARKETS

It has become a significant advantage to develop a complete trading framework for all assets backed by both trading *and* economic cycle systems. Naturally, there is a great deal of detail to this kind of institutional-level approach, but it is increasingly available to all investors.

The practice and management of this approach are also described in the McCullough video. This system has enabled Keith McCullough to build wealth without significant drawdowns. This shows how a Best Investor reviews and explains his whole trading/investing process.

SUMMARY

Active Investment Management is a precondition for optimal investing. Best Investors have to be constantly focused on their criteria. In order to achieve the best outcome for capital preservation and compounding, take the best advantage of opportunities, and efficiently manage risk, active management is a requirement, not an option.

However well-constructed a static portfolio is, it comes without real-time risk management and so is exposed to unacceptable drawdowns.

Cycle-based systems can provide important and timely information about optimal allocation. Combined with effective market price systems, they can transform the capability of investors to improve their performance.

The next and final chapter addresses these questions: How many models can you use together at the same time? How many ways can there be to reduce risk and increase alpha? Are there some clues about how to get the best research? Where does strategy come into this? How does this all work together in the best possible way?

CHAPTER 12

DECISIVE COMPREHENSIVE PROCEDURE FOR CONSISTENT PERFORMANCE

"Evolving is life's greatest accomplishment and its greatest reward."

—RAY DALIO

A Best Investor is committed to improving low risk and alpha performance to the point of obsession.[34] The quest never ends. New technology, methodologies, behaviors, and techniques are constantly being developed. New market conditions will also emerge. You must, therefore, consistently evolve. Never be static in what you use and how you use it, even while remaining true and consistent with the best process you have right now.

A good practitioner has clear Best Investor principles and objectives and just needs to focus on best execution. Best investing is the ability to put it all together so that acting in real time is instantaneous, conflict-free, and procedural. The more you can put together excellent systems and factors that you can apply to any investment idea, the more you will strengthen your conviction level on any trade and, in turn, what trades you choose and how and when you choose them. In this way, your probability of success should improve.

It stands to reason that when you can have ten factors aligned on any investment, you will have a greater level of conviction than with only two factors. How many models can you use at the same time? How do you put them

---

34   The image at the beginning of this chapter can be found at: Sandra Durcevic, "Why data driven decision making is your path to business success," April 16, 2019, https://www.datapine.com/blog/data-driven-decision-making-in-businesses/.

together? In research, the principle of strength in numbers is called "consilience," and it is key to best investing.

CONSILIENCE

In science and history, consilience (also known as "convergence" or "concordance" of evidence) means that when multiple unrelated sources of evidence are in agreement, the conclusion can be strong even when none of the individual sources is significantly so on its own.

Similarly, optimal investment involves finding not just individual approaches that have clear merit but also multiple systems with different methodologies that increase confirmation of an investment idea. The search and constant refinement of multiple methodologies add significant efficiency to achieving optimal investment management.

Moreover, there can be multiple levels to any decision, from macro down to micro levels. For example, TradeStops provides a complete money management system and continues to develop and extend its capabilities. Highly efficient return/risk management systems are embedded in both individual positions, as well as sector, factor, or macro positions for portfolio construction.

By having an effectively defined trend and risk factor for all levels of securities, it is possible to summarize the current status of all markets for broad consilience and to answer questions like these:

- Are global equities in an uptrend?
- Which countries have equities in an uptrend?
- Which market *sectors* are in an uptrend?
- Which market *factors* are in an uptrend?
- Which individual stocks are in an uptrend?

For example, if Microsoft's stock price (MSFT) is in an uptrend, that could be a good reason to buy, particularly if it is early in the uptrend. In addition, if high beta, technology, and global equities are also in uptrends, your conviction level could rise. Furthermore, if you are in a rising growth phase of the cycle, and three billionaires own the stock, and as many as five independent newsletters with a strong track record rate MSFT a buy, your conviction levels and understanding put this investment high on your list. All this data can be easily aggregated so that you can check which ideas have the strongest consilience or conviction behind them.

All this can transform your probability of successful outcomes.

TradeSmith lays this all out—from the macro down to the micro level. Most global stock markets were not in an uptrend when this chart was produced.

Market Outlook

75%
Markets in
Black Zone

- Australia
- Canada
- DOW 30
- Hong Kong
- Japan
- NASDAQ 100

- Russell 1000
- Russell 2000
- S&P 400
- S&P 500
- S&P 600
- United Kingdom

Trend characteristics can also be used at a micro level for portfolio construction and can tie in the many strategies a position is aligned with while showing which research notes are also analyzing the security. The risk factor and trend position can also be shown for both trade signals and position size calculation.

Trending Stocks

Ticker	SSI	Risk (VQ%)	Newsletters	Strategies
AAPL Apple	4m+	17.64%	5	
DIS Walt Disney-Dis	1w+	13.62%	5	2
FB Facebook-A	2w+	19.39%	4	2
MA Mastercard-A	7d	16.27%	1	3
NTES NetEase Sp ADR	11m+	28.49%	2	
WBA Walgreens Boots	3m+	17.16%	2	
WY Weyerhaeuser REI	5m+	16.42%	2	

These concepts can, of course, be applied to any portfolio, or even ideas about portfolio construction, and ensure that effective risk management is in place. For a clearer understanding of this, you can check out TradeSmith's knowledge base.[35]

RESEARCH

I focus on independent sources, who are sole providers of research and have a successful track record of ideas and results. The higher the quality of your sources, the better the flow of ideas.

To gain the deepest insight, you may also need to work with specialists. For example, given multiple issues with individual stock analysis, what factors are the most important for various stocks? And, not least, what most accurately constitutes a company's earnings? How aligned and authentic are the company's management, what shows up in their statements, and how are they delivered?

Forensic accounting can simplify a great deal, as the Best Investors confirm.

Anyone involved in US equity investment needs ongoing advice from a team that can deconstruct earnings and balance sheets with full research from first principles. While a

---

35 "Knowledge Base," Ideas by TradeSmith, https://ideas.tradesmith.com/knowledge-base/.

good analyst or fund manager should be able to do much of this work themselves, it is not possible to cover thousands of companies in any great detail in a timely fashion.

Be careful about earnings. According to forensic accountants at Altimetry:

"We are guided by the knowledge that US accounting guidelines—which American public companies are forced to follow—obscure the true results of a company's profitability, misleading investors."

Many investors may not be fully aware of this issue, but, of course, the Best Investors are:

"The net earnings figure...is not representative of the business at all."

—WARREN BUFFETT

"Analysis of reported earnings can mislead investors as to the real profitability of a business."

—SETH KLARMAN

Much more information is available on Altimetry's website.[36]

---

36 See "FAQs," Altimetry, https://altimetry.com/faq.

STRATEGY

In addition to using the investment tools and research discussed above, you need to be aware of market conditions where new factors may emerge, making some models more or less effective. So strategic thinking is essential as well.

A commitment to documenting market conditions and appropriate strategies are also important. Writing it down is a great discipline for any investor, as it forces clarity and quality of argumentation. It also provides transparency.

THE MARKET IN REAL TIME: A CASE STUDY

To show you how consilience works when it comes together across a full process, let's examine, as a case study, the situation in Q1 2020.

Extremes in both directions were experienced in Q1 2020—in sentiment, valuation, volatility, and price behavior. To be successful through this period, it was necessary to be fully aware of the risks and not distracted by the noise, emotion, and numerous opinions and advice of all the experts.

The year itself began highly uncertain—I published an article on January 2, 2020,[37] that I believed that investment conditions were already in three levels of crisis as

---

37   Chris Belchamber, "Q4 2019 Review. 3 levels of crisis," CB Investment Management, January 2, 2020, https://chrisbelchamber.com/q4-2019-review-3-levels-of-crisis/.

we entered the new decade. Then the novel coronavirus emerged, and it became apparent that there would be economic consequences. By the end of January 2020, Hedgeye's models were already signaling with high probability that **"both the US and Chinese economies will be in #Quad4 in Q2 of 2020."** In other words, the economic quadrant for the two largest economies in the world would experience falling growth *and* falling inflation into the second quarter of 2020.

So, the warning signs for equities were clear before the end of January: the fragility of investment conditions combined with the world's two biggest economies lining up for quad-four conditions (falling inflation and growth) created the most negative conditions for equities in the near term.

As signaled, the US equity market peaked more than two weeks later, on February 19, 2020, and fell over 34 percent over the next few weeks. For the second time in less than two years, the economic signal was available in advance and provided the opportunity to shift out of equities to avoid the worst conditions for equities immediately ahead.

With effective strategy and economic cycle and trading models, it was just a matter of procedure to change strategy and start shifting into new allocations in a timely fashion to at least minimize risks or even proactively position for a deep equity correction in the second half of Q1 2020.

For the second time in less than two years, there was a clear signal, in advance, that US equities were at high risk. Both times this signal was correct, and the two biggest US equity drawdowns since 2008 could have been avoided as a straightforward matter of process. This is how consilience across the full process can come together to operate as an opinion-free and emotion-free process for risk management, alpha, and continued compounding for the long term, in line with Best Investor criteria.

SUMMARY

Constant evolution is essential with constantly developing markets, techniques, and economic environments. If you're not moving forward, you're falling behind.

Tools, models, and the behavior of markets are always changing. While remaining true to your process and principles, the more wisdom you can bring to your checklist, software modeling, and investment-behavior experience, the better. This comes together through consilience, which will help you reach conviction about the best option available to you in a timely and effective manner.

In addition, research and writing strategies are also important for clarity, transparency, and accountability.

This all came together in Q1 of 2020 (just as it had for Q4

2018, as discussed in chapter 3). The strategic imperative for being ready for these crucially important drawdowns was published well in advance and time-stamped in June 2018, around three months in advance, and in January 2020.

When the mindset is well established from Part I, and there is great clarity about risk and return criteria from Part II, and you are strategically prepared for significant changes, and economic models signal a diametrically opposite change in the investment environment, an investor is on alert to take signals to start changing allocations well in advance of events, just as a matter of process. There was very little need to make much, if any, discretionary decisions. All the criteria for the decisions and execution to avoid these drawdowns were procedural and systematic.

CONCLUSION

"Learn how to see. Realize that everything connects to every-thing else."

—LEONARDO DA VINCI

From beginning to end, this book has laid out a grounded and coherent path through all the steps to bring any investor to a full understanding of what a Best Investor really is and how to benefit from this journey. This is a transformation toward higher long-term returns with lower risk, and it's not a paradox.

It started by developing and fortifying an effective mindset, so this can be practiced effectively.

"Avoiding loss should be the primary goal of every investor. This does not mean that investors should never incur the risk of any loss at all. Rather 'don't lose money' means that over several

years, an investment portfolio should not be exposed to appreciable loss of capital. While no one wishes to incur losses, you couldn't prove it from an examination of the behavior of most investors and speculators. The speculative urge that lies within most of us is strong; the prospect of free lunch can be compelling, especially when others have already seemingly partaken. It can be hard to concentrate on losses when others are greedily reaching for gains and your broker is on the phone offering shares in the latest 'hot' initial public offering. Yet the avoidance of loss is the surest way to ensure a profitable outcome."

—SETH KLARMAN

Here are the questions I asked in the introduction. Are your answers different now that you have read the book?

THE BIG INVESTMENT QUESTIONS
RISK AND RETURN

1. Does higher risk lead to higher return?
2. Do you need more than just return to measure whether your investment process is aligned with the Best Investors?
3. What part has risk and luck played in your return, and what part will they likely play in the future?

MEASUREMENT

1. What are the best practice measurements of your investment process and progress?

DECISION-MAKING

1. How far from optimal is your own investment thinking and decision process?
2. In investing, do you need to take charge of your own best interest? Can that be made simple?

OTHER STRATEGIC ELEMENTS

1. Do you see rules-based or systematic computer-driven investing as a useful addition?
2. Is passive investing aligned with the Best Investors?

The book has addressed all but the third question, and that's the one that matters now.

The gift from the Best Investors is that they have provided guidance through the labyrinth of the investment world. Without their deep insights, it might be impossible to carve out an optimal path through all the narratives, opinions, misdirection, and self-sabotage that all too often distract investors.

The Best Investors have toiled for decades to solve a

dynamic and complex puzzle full of unknowns and random, unforeseen events to come out far ahead in the end. This is no easy task, and it needs a great deal of clarity across a range of issues. It also deserves our respect and attention.

The most important parts of investing are often the most overlooked. The biggest problems that investors have come from their mindset and their confusion about the dynamics of risk and return.

Part I developed a mindset framework to clear away self-sabotage and misdirection. It explains the limitations of focusing solely on returns as the path to getting rich—a major error of oversimplifying a complex environment. Consequently, misallocation leads to unnecessary risk and luck playing a substantial role in their results. The Best Investors have higher priorities than return.

Part II showed the importance of focusing on risk and return/risk, rather than just return. It also explained the dynamics of risk and return and the key criteria for investing like the best. It also showed how easily measurable these criteria are for determining whether you are on track in real time with Best Investor metrics.

The assumption that only higher risk leads to higher long-term returns was exposed as a myth. What became apparent was that by lowering risk, you can find investment approaches that can show significant improvements in long-term returns. That's how the Best Investors realized how to compound their lower-risk high returns to achieve their outstanding long-term returns.

Part III developed investment techniques, favoring the "High Returns from Low Risk" approach. You learned there are limitations to passive or static allocation models. They fail to make the grade for Best Investors. Only active management can deliver optimal performance. You learned which models and combinations provide even greater effectiveness and efficiency. You learned how the best decisions could become high probability and procedural through an effectively developed investment mindset framework.

Now let's answer Question 3. Risk and luck play a part in everyone's investment outcomes, but the Best Investors minimize risk and luck as much as possible. Their top priorities are:

1. Capital preservation
2. High return/risk investing

As chapters 5 and 6 showed mathematically, these two objectives do not conflict. In fact, the metrics show they work together.

Multiple investment techniques show how you can repeatedly reach these objectives with a range of strategies. Now you know the best metrics to use to select investment strategies and ensure you stay on track in real time.

Far too many investors end up taking too much risk, poorly allocated, and without effective active management. In this case, risk and luck play far too great a role in their long-term investment performance.

At the end of your journey through this book, I hope you see a deeply grounded path to optimal long-term investing. It is within your reach. Now you understand how to use the same metrics and reporting requirements as the Best Investors. Now you can see how the Best Investors assess whether your capital is safe and is optimally compounding returns.

You've found the path to consequential long-term benefits, not just in terms of wealth, but also in lower stress and greater financial stability. You're in charge of your investing future, and you now know how to "Invest Like the Best."

BEST INVESTOR INSIGHT CHECKLIST

CHAPTER 1

Best Investors Insight 1: Take full responsibility for everything.

Best Investors Insight 2: Don't focus solely on returns.

Best Investors Insight 3: Don't assume you can know the future. Commit to thinking about the future by making decisions only through the lenses of humility and probability.

Best Investors Insight 4: Be aware of the ways in which your own investment process may be falling short. The extent of known cognitive biases is just an indication of how extensive this issue is.

CHAPTER 2

Best Investors Insight 5: Theory and assumptions can help a great deal in development, but investors need to be grounded in facts, evidence, math, and reality. What works in markets is behavioral economics and embracing complexity.

Best Investors Insight 6: Understand and then optimize your brain function.

Best Investors Insight 7: The Investment Mindset Framework develops rules to contain system one brain function while adding software systems to boost system two.

CHAPTER 3

Best Investors Insight 8: Software Investment Systems empower you in at least six different ways.

CHAPTER 4

Best Investors Insight 9: Beware of three types of risk: market, liquidity, and incentive.

Best Investors Insight 10: Experience and track record are a valuable initial requirement but insufficient without clearer metrics and ongoing real-time measurement. The experience of the management team and the size of returns are not exceptions.

Best Investors Insight 11: Even at the highest levels of investment management and across the whole financial industry, there is a pervasive intellectual and/or behavioral confusion about the balance between risk and return, both for accurate assessment and for setting investment objectives.

Best Investors Insight 12: Be aware of all conflicts of interest.

CHAPTER 5

Best Investors Insight 13: The only way investors can feel confident that they are on the path to multi-decade investment success is to adopt, and then demand, the right priorities and assessments.

Best Investors Insight 14: What should drive investment is expected return and risk management. Risk is the denominator of return/risk and has more impact on this calculation than return. Best Investors are risk-averse.

CHAPTER 6

Best Investors Insight 15: Best Investors have rejected the widely used theory that higher risk is linked to higher return (as shown in the previous chapter). Finding out more about the evidence and math of your underlying investment assumptions is strongly advised before you invest.

Best Investors Insight 16: Behavioral economics and evidence suggest that higher volatility generally corresponds with FALLING asset prices.

Best Investors Insight 17: To assess managers effectively, look at multiple years of compounded returns and additional metrics. Short-term returns tell you very little or can be completely misleading.

Best Investors Insight 18: Losses are devastating to long-term compounded returns; as a rule of thumb, an annual return needs twice the annual gain to make up for the loss.

Best Investors Insight 19: Real-time information on your portfolio risk and losses and how your manager addressed it is an essential tool that investors need to monitor in their own best interest.

Best Investors Insight 20: Risk is what you actually experience and need to manage in your portfolio in real time.

Best Investors Insight 21: Return variability also impacts compounding. This is a major limitation of any model projecting flat rates of compounding over multi-decade periods, as is standard practice in financial planning.

CHAPTER 7

Best Investors Insight 22: By the time your long-term returns turn out to be a great success or a complete failure, it's far too late to do anything about it. You can only tell whether you are on the right track, in time to alter course, by measuring the skill of the process from risk and return to risk.

Best Investors Insight 23: The risk and return performance grid provides the minimum information necessary for an investor to begin to understand the quality of the investment process in their own account.

CHAPTER 8

Best Investors Insight 24: Not only does passive investing involve many unresolved issues, but allocating to high risk within a passive allocation is also a highly questionable strategy.

ABOUT THE AUTHOR

CHRIS BELCHAMBER holds a Math MA from Oxford University. He has been an investment professional since 1984. His first investment book was published by Credit Suisse First Boston in 1988. He was recruited by JPMorgan in 1989 to run their UK Sterling Bond Sales and Trading and then focused on Proprietary Trading, where he was promoted to Managing Director.

He presented JPMorgan's UK Bond Market's development paper, endorsed by Margaret Thatcher, to the Bank of England in 1989. In 2003, he started his RIA in the US. He enjoys music, reading, writing, and almost any sport and is currently an active golfer.

Made in United States
North Haven, CT
18 June 2022

20362268R00125